1 Peter

Derek Cleave

Christian Focus

© Derek Cleave

ISBN 1 85792 337 5

Published in 1999 by
Christian Focus Publications
Geanies House, Fearn, Ross-shire
IV20 1 TW, Great Britain

Cover design by Donna Macleod

For a free catalogue of all our titles,
please write to the above address.

For details of our titles visit us on our web site
http://www.geanies.org.uk/cfp

Contents

Contents

INTRODUCTION

Introduction

Many of us would find ourselves more readily drawn to Simon Peter than to any of the other apostles. In Peter we see a man who failed his Lord on more than one occasion, and not all of his failures can be excused because of over-enthusiasm or impulse. There were some supreme high points but equally there were some miserable lows. This is the man who in the hour of his Master's greatest need, denied that he even knew him, and not once but three times!

So here is someone who vividly illustrates in his life the ever present potential for failure in any disciple of the Lord. In that sense he is certainly a man 'just like us' and we warm to him because of it.

At the same time we are encouraged to find that Peter was someone with whom the Lord was willing to exercise patience. He could see beyond his weaknesses. How many of us have been encouraged and reassured by the Lord's word to Peter, 'I have prayed for you' (Luke 22:32)? That prayer was answered when by God's grace, Peter was wonderfully transformed into a useful servant of Christ.

So when we think of Peter's natural characteristics we may well be amazed at the humble leadership he exercised in the early days of the Christian church. The humbling of that aggressive nature was brought about through his failure. He was made a far better leader because of his experience than he would have been without it.

In his introduction to 1 and 2 Peter, Eugene Peterson describes the Apostle in this way:

'The way Peter handled himself in that position of power is even more impressive than the power itself. He kept out of the centre of attention, he didn't parade his power, because he kept himself under the power of Jesus. He could have easily thrown around his popularity, power and position to try to take over, using his close association with Jesus to promote himself. But he didn't. Most people with Peter's gifts couldn't have handled it then *or* now, but he did. Peter is a breath of fresh air.'[1]

Sensible Christians know how susceptible we are to temptation, and how prone we are to failure. Yet our overriding desire is to be a useful servant of God and if the Lord can do in our lives something of what he did for Peter then surely there is hope for us. It is not difficult therefore for any of us to relate to this man.

Then the content of these epistles should also demand our attention. The message of both books is powerfully relevant to our day. They present basic and helpful information on living the Christian life. They provide vital teaching on the dangers of false doctrine and they give encouragement in the face of persecution.

Peter's intention is to provide an important balance between on the one hand, acknowledging the reality of suffering in its varied forms, with on the other, the need to live lives which please God. In the final assessment, *righteousness is ultimately more important than physical comfort or self gratification.* That kind of philosophy is of course diametrically opposed to the thinking of our present world. Inevitably this will mean believers suffering for righteousness' sake, but Peter's readers are to recognise that God always uses suffering in the believer's life for good. None of it is without value. And lest any should think that God himself is immune to suffering, Peter presents Christ's suffering for good as a supreme example for us.

Mercifully, the church in the West has not had to face organised persecution for some time, but who would be confident enough to suggest that this situation will continue *ad infinitum*? We were warned by the Lord that the world would hate us and the Apostle Paul confirms that fact by telling us that 'everyone who wants to live a godly life in Christ Jesus will be persecuted' (2 Tim. 3:12). There can be no escape from the repercussions of that verse if our desire is to live a life which pleases God. As Warren Wiersbe says, 'The only "comfortable" Christian will be a "compromising" Christian, and his comfort will be costly.'[2]

It is obvious from this first letter from Peter that his readers in the first century were already suffering for their faith and that still greater pressures were on the horizon. The signs are that this will be increasingly true for believers who will live in the twenty first century, therefore these epistles should be essential reading for us today.

There is no shortage of excellent commentaries on these New Testament books, but they must not be a substitute for reading the letters themselves. God has promised to bless his Word, not necessarily commentaries on it! These epistles are not long. Try reading each of them at one sitting. Peter tells us at the end of the first letter that he has written **briefly,... encouraging you and testifying that this is the true grace of God. Stand fast in it (5:12).**

The **true grace of God** has to be the answer to every spiritual need we confront. The more desperate our need, the deeper we will need to plumb the depths of God's grace for us. As Michael Bentley comments: 'One of the ways in which we can be ready for suffering is to learn more about the Christian faith.'[3]

Through the inspiration of the Spirit of God Peter knows what his readers will need and he comprehensively, yet concisely, covers the necessary ground.

To begin with, we must look in more detail at the **WHO**, **WHEN**, and **WHERE** of this Epistle.

WHO wrote the letter ?

The authorship of 1 Peter has hardly ever been in question. It claims simply to be the writing of the Apostle: **Peter, an apostle of Jesus Christ (1:1).** Further confirmation of this is provided when he tells us that he was **a witness of Christ's sufferings (5:1).**

It is important to realise that this epistle was accepted as

Petrine by those we refer to as the 'fathers' of the early church. These were early Christian writers some of whom it was believed had contact with the apostles. Their writings often included reference to New Testament letters and we can certainly be sure that they would have been very thorough in testing their authenticity.

During this period of the Christian church many other letters were circulating some of which purported to come from Peter. Many were rejected, yet this one received universal acceptance. Just about the only scholar to reject it was Marcion, and he rejected it because it *was* Peter's! He was only prepared to accept Paul's writings.

Any real criticism of the authorship has come in the last two centuries. A number of objections have been raised. Some suggest that it has overtones of Pauline teaching which would it is suggested, have made it impossible for Peter to be its author. Critics believe he would not have had access to that material. Others say that the historical background seems to suggest a time later than the persecution under Nero, which again would eliminate the possibility of Peter being its author. Still others feel that it lacks the authenticity of a personal companion of the Lord. It is too self effacing. If it is Peter and he did have first hand knowledge of Christ's earthly life why not press home this unique qualification more strongly?

None of these objections can set aside the strong support for Petrine authorship from the vast majority of Christian writers of the earliest century. Critical scholars may question Peter's authorship of the book but they have never made any satisfactory alternative suggestions as to who the author might have been!

One issue does perhaps demand a little more attention. In the early days of the Christian church, Peter and his associate John are considered by the Sanhedrin to be 'unlearned and ignorant men' (Acts 4:13 AV), so how, we are asked, could Peter have written this letter in Greek and with such elegant touches?

We do not of course have to accept the Sanhedrin's biased view! But even if their assessment of these two men was correct we should understand what they meant.

Firstly, the Authorised Version translation of this verse can be misunderstood. The New International Version provides a better twentieth century translation when it refers to Peter and John as being 'unschooled, ordinary men'. They were laymen without formal training, but they were certainly not illiterate. Greek was the second language after Aramaic, and spoken widely. Peter would also have been extremely familiar with the Septuagint (the Greek translation of the Old Testament). He certainly quotes extensively from it. The Septuagint was the standard version of the Scriptures for the majority of early Christians.

Greek language and culture had invaded every area of Jewish life, and Acts 6 shows a strong Grecian element in the church in Jerusalem. It is not surprising therefore that those involved in ministry to the Gentiles should be so familiar with the language of the day.

To further overcome the 'problem' of Peter's inability to write this epistle there is another interesting hypothesis. In 5:12 Peter refers to Silas in the following way: **With the help of Silas, whom I regard as a faithful brother, I have written to you ...** This is generally believed to be the Silas who was associated with Paul. But was Silas simply the bearer of this letter? Perhaps he was also the *amanuensis* or secretary to whom it was dictated, or did he even have some share in its composition?

In Acts 15:22 Silas, together with Judas, was sent to Gentile believers in Antioch with a letter from the Apostles in Jerusalem. It is clear that on that occasion they were merely bearers of the letter. Why is a similar term not used in Peter's epistle if Silas was no more than a carrier of this letter?

History shows us that secretaries could be given considerable power. The author of a letter would convey an idea of the message he wished to convey and leave the secretary to draw up the argument. The author might then revise it and perhaps add a few words of his own before signing it. It was recognised as his letter and it was guaranteed by him.

Silas would certainly have had a deep interest in the people of Asia Minor, who were to be the recipients of this letter. There seems nothing objectionable therefore about the cooperation of Silas on the epistle, but this must remain a hypothesis.

It is generally agreed that the letter was written from Rome. The allusion in **5:13** can apply to a number of alternatives. The Babylon in Mesopotamia, a military post on the Nile, or the city of Rome itself.

The first suggestion seems to have little substance since we do not even know if Peter stayed there. The Eastern Church has never claimed Peter for themselves, except on the basis of this verse!

The second was little more than a fortress and it seems unlikely that Peter would have a base there.

However most commentators agree that references to Babylon in the Revelation are references to Rome (e.g.14:8; 17:5), and it was a commonly understood code name used by Christians, though there was probably no reason for Peter to use it in that way.

Might he therefore have been speaking of Babylon in a metaphorical sense? Babylon was seen as the place of exile, and by using this word Peter may be simply linking believers in Rome with those in Asia Minor as those 'in exile', whereas their true home is in heaven.

WHEN was it written ?

The main clue we have to dating the epistle is the very obvious teaching on suffering, even death to be expected by believers. This would link it to Emperors who were instrumental in acute persecution of believers. It must therefore be either during the reign of: (1) Trajan 98-117 or (2) Domitian 81-96 or (3) Nero 54-68. If this letter is indeed the work of Peter as we have sought to show, then some of these dates are virtually impossible.

The most satisfactory of the above alternatives is a date of 63 or 64, just prior to the spread of Nero's persecution. This began in Rome and eventually covered the whole empire. If we accept the Nero date, it is almost certain that Paul is already dead and James too. Mark and Silas have perhaps turned from Paul to help Peter; one of them in the gospel (Mark) and the other in the epistle. We cannot say for sure. Historical tradition suggests that within two years, Peter had also been put to death in the way the Lord had indicated to him (John 21:18,19).

WHERE was the letter sent ?

Who were to be the recipients of this letter? We are given some addresses in 1:1. Certain regions of Asia Minor are not mentioned here e.g. Lystra, Derbe, Iconium and Pisidian Antioch. Those were areas covered by Paul during his missionary journeys. Are the districts Peter outlines those parts of Asia Minor not as thoroughly evangelised by Paul?

We recall that Paul had been restrained from going into Bithynia. Was that because others were to have this responsibility (Acts 16:7)? It seemed to be a principle of Paul's ministry that he did not 'double up' on someone else's work (Rom. 15:20).

In any case, the areas Peter refers to are the northernmost parts of Asia Minor, roughly the geographical area we know as Turkey today.

Remember too that when Peter preached on the Day of Pentecost there were those present from Cappadocia, Pontus and Asia who would have heard the gospel, responded to it and taken the message back to their own areas. They could have been instrumental in the founding of the church in those places.

But there is some question as to what background these

people had and the following alternatives must be considered.

The first suggestion is that they were native born Jews converted to the Christian faith. Certainly the phrase **strangers in the world (1:1)** has strong Jewish overtones. However other references in the epistle would seem to contradict this view.

Could an exclusively Jewish readership be described as having an **empty way of life (1:18)**? And what of the description of their previous life? **For you have spent enough time in the past doing what pagans choose to do – living in debauchery, lust, drunkenness, orgies, carousing and detestable idolatry (4:3)!**

How could this kind of life, even if it were true of a backslidden Jew, be said to have been **handed down to you from your forefathers (1:18)**.

A second proposition is that they were Gentiles. There are references in the epistle that suggest that those who previously were not Christian were idolaters (see above 4:3). This is not the language which would be used of Jews.

The fact that there are so many references to the Old Testament is not in itself an argument against a Gentile readership since Paul followed a similar pattern in some of his writings.

The third alternative is that they were Christians converted from both Jews and Gentiles. This would fit in with the language used, where there are asides to both those who were Jews and those who had been pagans.

This option may be a convenient fence to sit on, but I believe the weight of argument favours a predominantly Gentile readership.

Sulpicus Severus, the Roman historian, tells us that Peter was crucified during the reign of Nero, after the fire that destroyed half of the city. Stuart Briscoe paints a graphic picture of those days: 'The emperor, whose unpopularity had been well earned, was widely suspected of arson but managed to divert suspicion to the Christians, who were easy prey for his malicious slander. They were horribly persecuted even to the extent that "new kinds of death were invented"; they were "devoured by dogs" and some were "set apart ... that when the day came to a close, they should be consumed to serve for light." Eventually it was decreed by Rome that it was "unlawful to be a Christian." [4]

How much of this could have been foreseen by Peter we cannot know, but it was to minister to this kind of situation that he wrote in such a positive way.

Paul has been called the apostle of faith, John the apostle of love and Peter the apostle of hope. This epistle confirms that assessment.

References

1. Eugene H Peterson, *The Message: The New Testament in Contemporary English*, Navpress, 1993, p. 486.
2. W. Wiersbe, *Be Hopeful*, Victor Books, 1982, p. 9.
3. Michael Bentley, *Living for Christ in a Pagan World*, Evangelical Press, 1990, p. 15.
4. Stuart Briscoe, *Holy Living in a Hostile World*, Shaw, 1982, p. 2.

CHAPTER ONE

OUR SALVATION

Letters in the first century began by introducing the author. This one is no exception. **Peter's** name provides variations on a theme! His given name was Simon or Simeon, but it was the Lord who gave him this extra name and indicated its significance (John 1:42, cf. Matt. 16:18). Petros is the Greek form of the name, meaning 'a stone'. The Aramaic, which was Peter's native language, would be Cephas. So in the New Testament he is variously referred to as Simon, Simon Peter or Peter.

This was the Galilean fisherman who by the grace of God became one of the earliest leaders of the Christian church.

an apostle of Jesus Christ. A simple yet magnificent declaration. He is an apostle; his authority has a divine source, but he lays no claim to be the leader of that unique body of God-appointed men, or even to set himself above these fellow believers to whom he writes. This sets the tone for the epistle in which the author keeps himself firmly in the background. For some this confirms Petrine authorship, for others it presents a question mark.

He had been the spokesman for the disciples in confessing Jesus as 'the Christ, the Son of the living God' and at that time received the Lord's special promise concerning the building of his church (Matt. 16:16,18). He had preached the first Christian sermon on the Day of Pentecost and seen thousands repent and believe and become some of the first members of that Church to which Christ had referred (Acts 2). His name is always first when the apostles are listed.

But Peter clearly understands that the Church of Jesus Christ is not built on him alone. Rather the basis of the church is the unique foundation of the apostles and prophets. Paul confirms this truth when he speaks of the church as 'God's household, built on the foundation of the apostles and prophets, with Christ Jesus himself as the chief cornerstone. In him the whole building is joined together' (Eph. 2:20). Just as God's people of the Old Testament were founded on the twelve tribes of Israel so the 'new Israel', the church, is built on the divinely chosen and gifted agents of God's revelation: the prophets of the Old Testament and their New Testament equivalents, the apostles. That Church comprises as its equal members all who have made a similar confession to Peter's, *having received a similar revelation from God* (see again Matt. 16:16,17).

An 'apostle' signifies a person sent by another, a messenger or a representative. Might there be a twofold meaning here? First and primarily, he was unquestionably sent by Jesus Christ, but was he not also sent to serve and proclaim Jesus Christ?

The phrase **of Jesus Christ** is not used as a suffix to any other office in the church. Apostleship was a distinctive appointment, and in its New Testament sense confined to the first century. It seems to be clear that a requirement of a New Testament apostle was that he had seen the risen Lord (Acts 1:21-22; 1 Cor. 9:1).

Peter does not need any added confirmation of his apostleship, unlike Paul (cf. 1 Cor. 1:1; 2 Cor. 1:1; Gal. 1:1; Eph. 1:1), since Peter's claim to the title has never been in question.

It is important to underline again the grace of God in elevating Peter to this position. This is the Peter who denied Jesus Christ with curses but who is now a representative of, and a messenger from, this same Christ. How significant were the angel's words to the women on that resurrection morning 'Go, tell his disciples *and Peter*' (Mark 16:7). This was and is 'amazing grace.'

to God's elect, strangers in the world, scattered throughout Pontus, Galatia, Cappadocia, Asia and Bithynia. Peter has been economical when speaking of himself, but he says much more about his readers. As to their geographical location, they are Christians in the area covering much of what we call Turkey today, the northern parts of that vast district of Asia Minor. The actual order of place names may have been the route that the carrier of the letter would take.

In contrast, many of Paul's letters were sent to a local church, but here Peter writes to a much wider congregation. Paul often dealt with specific problems within a church; Peter has a much broader purpose. **I have written to you ... encouraging you and testifying that this is the true grace of God. Stand fast in it (5:12).** The kind of suffering which his readers are to face does not always lead to victory and success. There are those in every generation who have failed under testing. Peter certainly knew that! Therefore these believers need not only encouragement but the challenge to **stand fast**.

Their relationship with God is underlined first of all. They are **God's elect** which links closely with verse 2: **who have been chosen**. And they are also referred to as **strangers in the world, scattered throughout...**

This latter expression usually refers to Jews living in Gentile lands. His readers are believers and as such are strangers or 'aliens' because essentially they are passing through (Greek, *parepidemos*). Old fashioned though it is, the word 'sojourners' would perhaps provide a more accurate understanding of the Greek since some of his readers have lived all their lives in that area, and in that sense are not 'strangers' as we understand that term. The word translated 'strangers' here is a different one to that used in verse 17 where the emphasis is more on remaining in a land but not taking up citizenship there. 'Sojourners' suggests that these believers are only temporary residents wherever they reside; their home is in heaven. However much they are rejected, wherever they are living on earth, they do *belong* somewhere!

The word for 'scattered' is the word *diaspora* or 'Dispersion' and is often used of Jews in a Gentile environment. These two phrases seem to present a strong argument for a Jewish readership, but though Christian Jews may be among his readers, there are too many other references in this epistle which would point away from an exclusively Jewish readership.

This makes Peter's initial declaration all the more amazing. As a God-fearing Jew he would not have a kind word to say about a Gentile, and certainly not in the area of religion. A traditional Jew would begin his daily prayer by thanking God that he had not made him a Gentile and secondly that he had not been made a woman! We remember the significance of Peter's unwillingness to obey God when on the rooftop prior to his visit with Cornelius (Acts 10). At that time Gentiles being 'God's elect' would have been furthest from his thoughts.

Now he knows that the essential ingredient in 'true religion' is an individual's relationship with Jesus Christ the Son of God. When you belong to the Son of God, you belong to the people of God from whatever stock you may have come. Peter surely remembered the Lord's words, 'Do not call anything impure that God has made clean' (Acts 10:15).

Whoever his readers are, Peter honours them with the title **God's elect.** The New International Version has added **God's** which is not in the Greek. This serves to confirm the link with the Old Testament teaching on the unique position which Jews in that dispensation enjoyed. New Testament believers can enjoy a similar designation. So part of Peter's purpose in writing this letter is because his readers, **God's elect,** are not living in peace and safety but **scattered**, and in an hostile environment.

Edmund Clowney remarks: 'Peter is writing a travellers' guide for Christian pilgrims. He reminds them that their hope is anchored in their homeland. They are called to endure alienation as strangers, but they have a heavenly citizenship and destiny.'[1]

who have been chosen according to the foreknowledge of God the Father (v. 2). Now here is the doctrine of election clearly stated. An all-knowing God does of course possess forward knowledge about every inhabitant of the earth, but the **foreknowledge of God** which Peter refers to here is much more than prior information. God did not simply predict their conversion – he predetermined it.

The correct understanding of the word **foreknowledge** includes that idea of predetermination. These believers had been selected according to the sovereign will of God the Father. As Davids suggests: 'The cause of their salvation is not that they reached out to a distant God, but that God chose to relate to them and form them into a people, his people. Thus the use of the term "Father" for God is especially apt, for it indicates the loving concern with which God chose to know them.'[2]

Remember, too, that we believe that Peter is also addressing Gentiles! The Old Testament emphasises God's special choosing of the Jewish nation. Now Peter is underlining the point that Gentiles were not added to make up the numbers following the failure of Jews to respond wholeheartedly to the gospel of Jesus Christ. Rather Gentile Christians were among those chosen from eternity past to receive the blessings of salvation. What a glorious truth with which to assure these believers. These are the things they need to hear in their current situation. Essentially 'election here means the selecting them out of the world and joining them to the fellowship of the people of God'.

We believe that God is the One who we are told, 'works out *everything* in conformity with the purpose of his will' (Eph. 1:11), but in this context it is all about God choosing *people*.

Paul majors on this great theme of election by informing us that 'those God foreknew he also predestined... and those he predestined, he also called; those he called, he also justified; those he justified, he also glorified' (Rom. 8:29,30). One infallible step here is securing the next infallible step. In that passage foreknowledge leads without fail to glorification; everyone foreknown in that way will be glorified. But since it is obvious that not every individual will ultimately be glorified, therefore not everyone is foreknown in the precise sense that Paul suggests here. The apostle implies more than a simple advance knowledge.

Peter applies the word **foreknowledge** in just the same

way, to indicate that these Gentiles were included with the people of God before time began, because of the personal love which God had set upon them (Eph. 1:4-5; cf. Amos 3:2; 1 Cor. 8:3). The love of God is always the cause of God's favour toward his children in every generation.

This is the underlying security which every true believer can enjoy, and when the pressure increases Peter's readers will certainly need to be reassured of that fact.

through the sanctifying work of the Spirit. The will of God the Father is accomplished through the activity of the Spirit (2 Thess. 2:13). The root of the word for **sanctifying** includes the idea of cutting or dividing, which leads to our understanding of the biblical concept of separation. So the Spirit of God sanctifies, or sets apart, those whom God has chosen, so far as their allegiance and affection is concerned, though they remain in this world. The same Spirit will also be instrumental in the cleansing necessary for sustained fellowship with a holy God, and for that daily walk of separation before God.

for obedience to Jesus Christ. This is the design for which they have been chosen by God and sanctified by the Spirit. The primary evidence of unbelief is disobedience to God (Isa. 53:6; Heb. 4:6,11). Therefore obedience to God will be the evidence of the work of the Spirit, and the proof that we are **God's elect** and **chosen**. Henry Ward Beecher divided people into two categories: the 'whosoever wills' and the 'whosoever won'ts'. We can tell which we are by a simple test. Have we become obedient to him?

But though we *are* called to a life of obedience surely here, Peter is emphasising that initial obedience necessary to salvation; the **obeying** (of) **the truth** mentioned in verse 22.

So in these three phrases he provides a Trinitarian basis for our salvation. Following the Sovereign choice of the Father and the setting apart by the Spirit, the Christian life begins when we obey the truth by repenting of sin and turning in faith to Jesus Christ.

And the means by which we can be cleansed? **sprinkling by his blood**. Peter reaches back to the sacrificial system employed in the Old Testament. Not now the sprinkling of the blood of an animal but rather that of the lifeblood of Jesus Christ (Heb. 10:5-7). The death and resurrection of the Son of God was sufficient to absolve our debt to God by making atonement for our sins, thus turning aside the wrath of God on sin and so providing the ground for our justification. So extensive was the merit of Christ's sacrifice that through it God is not only able to deal with the past, but also to provide for our present and future need (Heb. 10:22; 12:24).

In his great hymn *Rock of Ages* Augustus Toplady recognised the comprehensive cleansing provided through the death of Christ when he wrote:

> Let the water and the blood,
> From Thy riven side which flowed,
> Be of sin the *double cure*,
> Cleanse me from its *guilt and power*.

So in this verse Peter states clearly the part each Person of the Trinity plays in the salvation of sinners.

Grace and peace be yours in abundance. The Greek and Hebrew greeting would appeal to all his readers. Bentley says that 'Peace was a characteristic of the Old Covenant; it spoke of well-being. Grace is the watchword of the New Covenant; it speaks of the free unmerited favour of God.'[3]

In fact the phrase was probably a common Christian greeting. It was certainly familiar to Jews because of its popular use in the temple (Num. 6:22-27). We find it repeated throughout the New Testament.

Grace in the biblical sense is the free favour of God toward those who have forfeited it. I remember hearing Stuart Briscoe say: 'Justice is getting what you deserve. Mercy is not getting all you deserve. Grace is getting what you don't deserve.'

Peace is that inner pleasure we experience because of the exercise of God's grace toward us. It has been said that 'peace is not the absence of trouble, but the presence of Christ'. The disciples found this to be true when they were in their boat on Galilee. They still had to face a violent storm; the difference from previous occasions was that Jesus was with them and was able to say, 'Be still!' (Mark 4:39). These first century believers would need just such an assurance.

Peter's wish is that they should be immersed in the blessings of grace and peace. May they **be yours in abundance** he says. As Ellicott remarks, 'There are *some* good things of which we cannot have too much'.[4]

In truth this greeting sums up Peter's intentions for this letter. His desire is that they may more fully understand God's grace toward them, and understanding that, they might know his peace in their trials.

1. SALVATION'S CHARACTER (verses 3 -9)

Peter immediately offers praise to God for such a great salvation: **Praise be to the God and Father of our Lord Jesus Christ! (v. 3).** This is a similar outburst of praise to that used by the Apostle Paul at the beginning of his letter to the Ephesian church.

The praise is offered to God but not to a God who is remote, because he **the Father of** *our* **Lord Jesus Christ**. This is the Messiah appointed by God, but he performs his duties in *our* interest and for *our* benefit!

Peter identifies at once two blessings we can experience through this great salvation. A new birth and a living hope. Both of these are far beyond human reach.

In his great mercy has given us a new birth. God is the Father of all mankind in a creatorial sense but he has now made us his children in a higher and better sense.

This 'gift' of new birth is exactly that! It is a gift because we cannot hope to pay for it or work for it. God **has given us a new birth** that is entirely of his mercy and not due to any merit accumulated by ourselves.

When Jesus met Nicodemus he had 'religion'; his job was to teach it! But what he possessed, albeit sincerely, was mainly head knowledge which could never address his real need. So ignorant was he in understanding spiritual truth he was unable to follow the teaching of Jesus. The Lord knew that his deepest need was for a new birth, and that there could be no alternative. '*Unless* a man is born again, he cannot see the kingdom of God.... You *must* be born again,' Jesus told him (John 3:3,7). To be 'born again' means literally to be born 'from above'. It is a miracle of God, performed by his Spirit, who transforms the nature of the sinner and brings that individual into the divine family. We can no more contrive the new birth, than we could engineer our physical birth (John 1:12-13). Belonging to a divine family means that in every sense God is truly 'our Father in heaven'.

Added to this blessing is the foundation for all Christian hope, what Peter calls the '*living* hope' and that foundation is **the resurrection of Jesus Christ from the dead**.

Everything Jesus said, and everything he did, was confirmed by his resurrection. Paul says that he 'was declared with power to be the Son of God *by his resurrection from the dead*' (Rom. 1:4). This momentous event in history is a pledge that those who belong to him will also be raised to new life (see for example John 11:25; Rom. 8:11; 1 Cor. 15:20f.). Without this assurance our position is hopeless. Paul says: 'If Christ has not been raised, your faith is futile; you are still in your sins' (1 Cor. 15:17).

Is it any wonder that Peter praises God? God has loved us to the extent that he has *guaranteed* us eternal life. So the promise that we have through the new birth and resurrection of Christ is **a living hope**. Wiersbe points out: 'True Christian hope is more than "hope so." It is confident assurance of future glory and blessing.'[5] We can know that, as Chuck Swindoll says, 'As difficult as some pages of our life may be, nothing that occurs to us on earth falls into the category of "the final chapter".'[6]

Hope is faith as it looks forward, because we know that
when God promises something, it will happen. There is not
the slightest possibility that it will fail to come to pass. The
writer to the Hebrews says that this hope is 'an anchor for the
soul, firm and secure' (Heb. 6:19). An anchor gives stability
to an object which is at the mercy of instability. That was
certainly true of conditions surrounding the believers to whom
Peter is writing. Martyrdom was an integral part of everyday
life. Every week a relative or a friend would be taken.
Christians found no security in anything around them so they
hung on to the promises of Christ. They had a living hope!
And there was more!

**and into an inheritance that can never perish, spoil or
fade – kept in heaven for you (v. 4).** Here is another
tremendous blessing we can anticipate through the mercy of
God. The new birth provides us with a legacy. This is an
additional aspect of the 'living hope' referred to in the
previous verse.

The inheritance was a truth particularly relevant to the Jew.
In the Old Testament the inheritance was the appointed
portion or lot to be possessed in Canaan by every one of God's
people (e.g. Ps. 37:11, 29). But the inheritance here is unique
because it is **kept in heaven**. The word 'kept' is a perfect
participle which confirms the fact that the inheritance already
exists and is being guarded in a safe place.

As a result of this, three negatives can be employed. It
cannot be corrupted from inside or outside, nor will it fade
away. Stuart Briscoe informs us that he delights in three point
sermons which have alliterative headings, so he feels he has
a kindred spirit with Peter who describes the inheritance as
follows: *aphthartos* (incorruptible), *amiantos* (undefiled),
amarantos (unfading)![7]

Many of the 'things' which fill our lives and which are
often thought to be valuable don't fit that criteria at all. They
are corruptible, defiled and they *do* fade, and if we set our
heart on such things we will end up disappointed and

disillusioned. But none of this applies to God's salvation.

Jesus had told his disciples to 'store up ... treasures in heaven, where moth and rust do not destroy, and where thieves do not break in and steal' (Matt. 6:20). Peter assures his readers that this is what they have. This fullness of salvation, has been carefully kept, put aside or 'reserved' (AV) **in heaven** and is waiting to be claimed, and it is **for you** says Peter. It could not be more personal!

Perhaps you have had the embarrassment of thinking that a hotel room or an airline ticket had been reserved for you, only to be told that there had been a mistake. With this reservation in such safe keeping, we can be sure that there will be no embarrassment or disappointment.

who through faith are shielded by God's power until the coming of the salvation that is ready to be revealed in the last time (v. 5). Not only can Peter's readers anticipate the inheritance of complete salvation waiting for them, but right now they are protected by the power of God. They can focus on the fact that not only is the inheritance preserved; so are the inheritors! God not only protects our future, but he also shields us in the present. Though two different words are used for the idea of the keeping of the treasure and the guarding of the individual, there is a nice balance in Peter's mind here.

The idea of being shielded or guarded is a military metaphor popular in the Scriptures (Gen. 15:1; Phil. 4:7; cf. Rom. 8:31-39). We are within the garrison and there are powerful raiding forces outside, yet we are safe because God himself is guarding the perimeter.

The ultimate reason why any Christian should think that he will reach heaven and enjoy salvation is because he or she is surrounded by the power of God. Our enemies are numerous and they are powerful and of ourselves we have insufficient strength to reach our goal. Here is the certainty! We **are shielded by God's power**!

But the deliverance, like so much else in the believer's

life, is **through faith**. This shielding or keeping is not an exercise of God's power independent of ourselves. His power encourages faith in our hearts and as we have faith in God and his promises, so we are safe.

And we are safe **until the coming of the salvation**. The salvation must refer not only to an initial rescue from sin but from all the repercussions of sin. Peter prompts his readers to look forward to the day when sin's trials and temptations, its struggles and persecutions will end. I believe that here he is looking at the very final scene in God's great act of salvation. Notice that we are shielded '*until* the coming of the salvation', which implies that whatever happens then we no longer need shielding!

When do we experience that fullness of our salvation? In particular it is **to be revealed in the last time**. Saved not only from the penalty of sin, that is the guilt of sin in the past; the current power of sin in the present, but also then, delivered from the very presence of sin. The Bible often encourages us by speaking of the events we can anticipate during a period variously called 'the last time', 'the great day', 'that day' or 'the last days'. Those events, including resurrection and judgment, will be initiated by nothing less than the coming again of Jesus Christ. The final scene in redemption will be enacted. That tremendous moment is still another ingredient in the believer's 'living hope.'

In this you greatly rejoice, though now for a little while you may have had to suffer grief in all kinds of trials (v. 6). Even in the midst of their difficulties this hope causes them to rejoice, such is the greatness of their salvation. It is the backcloth to their pain. Joy in the circumstances they are facing has to be the real thing, because unlike the superficial happiness which the world experiences, his readers' joy is not dependent in the final analysis on earthly happenings!

There is of course no joy in pain of itself, but in God's providence there is always profit in suffering for righteousness' sake. They must believe that God is in the 'all things' Paul speaks of in Romans 8:28, and that belief will lift them above any hasty judgment of daily happenings.

When Peter speaks of this joy he uses the Greek term *agalliasthai*, which has strong eschatological tones. He uses the same word again in verse 8 and in 4:13. As Hillyer points out it is literally an 'out of this world' kind of joy.[8]

In pointing to **a little while** Peter emphasises the brevity of their earthly trials when compared to their eternal reward. Paul also spoke of '*momentary* troubles' (2 Cor. 4:17).

Trials is a good translation of the Greek. *Pierasmos* here means not the inner wrestling with evil inclination but undeserved suffering from without. This new 'sect' encouraged suspicion in society because so little was known about them. They kept themselves to themselves and often through ignorance were unjustly accused of a variety of 'crimes'. For example there were question marks concerning their special feasts. Reference to eating Christ's body and drinking his blood caused great disturbance. Their emphasis on 'love for the brethren' was also misunderstood by some.

All kinds of trials have caused them to **suffer grief**. This is a helpful acknowledgement that earthly trials are real and cause grief and that they are varied, *(poikilos)* or literally 'multi-coloured' (notice also the same word is used in 4:10). Peter does not suggest that these trials should be trivialised; it does not make us more 'spiritual' to dismiss them as if they did not exist. They can cause deep physical and mental distress – his readers *have* suffered grief. But God can 'match' these multi-coloured trials with his 'multi-coloured' grace. And these are the ideal circumstances for true Christian joy to be experienced and expressed.

In suffering we often ask, 'Why?' Peter addresses that cry: **These have come so that your faith – of greater worth than gold, which perishes even though refined by fire – may be proved genuine and may result in praise, glory and honour when Jesus Christ is revealed (v. 7).**

Here is a primary purpose of trials in the Christian's life: **that your faith ... may be proved genuine...** Peter compares their trials with the test applied to gold. Gold is a precious metal in man's eyes, and its value warrants a stringent test. But faith is much more precious in God's sight and so demands an even more rigorous examination. Stibbs comments: 'Just as men use fire to distinguish between true gold and counterfeit, so God uses trials to distinguish genuine faith from superficial profession.'[9] Warren Wiersbe confirms that when he says that 'A faith that cannot be tested cannot be trusted'.[10] God uses trials to bring out the best in us, whereas the devil hopes that they will bring out the worst in us.

Therefore we should not be surprised by trials since they are divinely ordered (See also 4:12). Jesus told us that in the world we would have trouble (John 16:33). The Epistle to the Hebrews emphasises that God tests through trials (Heb. 12). James speaks of the testings that come from God (James 1:2) and Paul has much to say about suffering (e.g. Rom. 8:18). Here Peter is expressing similar truths.

We must also remember that trials are not only divinely ordered; they are also divinely controlled. Wiersbe again: 'When God permits His children to go through the furnace, He keeps His eye on the clock and His hand on the thermostat.'[11] (See also 1 Corinthians 10:13).

So trials prove the genuineness of faith, remove the impurities from our lives and centre our faith on Christ alone.

The **praise, honour and glory** of which Peter speaks and which will result from this testing of genuine faith will go both to the Lord *and* to the believer! We often speak of 'praising God' and certainly 'honour and glory' belong to him alone but notice the context of these words? Peter is referring to their proven faith and it seems that in the spirit of Matthew 25:21, 23: 'Well done, good and faithful servant', the Lord gives praise where it is due. It could also be said that he, the Lord, also gives honour and glory which belongs to him by right, to those who have demonstrated these attributes of God in their own lives and which he now graciously shares with them (see Rom. 2:7,10; 1 Cor. 10:31).

'Therefore judge nothing before the appointed time; wait till the Lord comes. He will bring to light what is hidden in darkness and will expose the motives of men's hearts. *At that time each will receive his praise from God*' (1 Cor. 4:5).

All of this is enjoyed **when Jesus Christ is revealed**, that is, at his Second Coming.

Stibbs points out that the word **revealed** is 'not the "coming" of someone previously absent but the visible unveiling of someone who has been all the time spiritually and invisibly present.'[12] By using this word Peter is expressing the idea that the presence and power of Christ, already present, will one day be openly demonstrated on this earth.

Though you have not seen him, you love him (v. 8). All of their joys, and ours too – are not in the future. It is possible to experience rich fellowship with the Lord here and now, even though we have not and cannot see him! Jesus said to Thomas who wanted to see before he would believe, 'Blessed are those who have not seen and yet have believed' (John 20:29). The eye of faith sees very clearly.

A person does not always have to see someone with their eyes in order to love them. A blind husband can love his wife though he has never seen her. Christians have not personally seen the Lord, yet they have heard about him and through the Word of God, the Bible, have come to know and appreciate the Word of God, the Son. Knowing him by faith and not by sight, they recognise more fully the benefits of his love for them, and so learn to love him ever more deeply. A realisation of the depth of his love for us will help to take the sting out of suffering.

and even though you do not see him now, you believe in him. Faith makes invisible things real and means that we can act with the same degree of certainty as if we had seen them. Our conviction about Jesus Christ as Saviour is as real and certain as if we had seen him with our physical eyes. For these believers, the most important things are not what they can see around them but the One they love with the eye of faith. If we love him then we can trust him and that can turn a trial into a triumph.

and are filled with an inexpressible and glorious joy. **Inexpressible** is unspeakable. This joy is unspeakable in the sense that it is hard to explain because it cannot be related to outward circumstances. It focuses on Christ and not on our condition. This joy is present because they '*believe* **in him**'. To do that is always the most effective antidote to trials and since that defies human logic and is so unlike the unbeliever's response to trial, it is 'inexpressible'.

It is also a taste of glory – it is a **glorious joy**. Believers are able to experience joy of the same kind as that which they will experience in heaven. 'The happiness of heaven will be but an expansion and prolongation and a purifying of that which believers have here' (Barnes).[13]

for you are receiving the goal of your faith, the salvation of your souls (v. 9). Here is the reason for their joy. This is the believers' ultimate assurance; we anticipate the salvation of our souls. Peter uses the word 'soul' (*psyche*) to refer to the total person not simply to distinguish between body and soul. His use here is typical of Hebrew and therefore of his 'Bible', the Septuagint (the Greek translation of the Old Testament).

The word **'goal'** is better than 'end' because it means consummation not conclusion. There is absolutely no doubt that they are going to be saved – in fact it could be said that they are already! That is why Peter can refer in the present tense to **receiving**. The Christian can at one and the same time, speak of having 'been saved', of 'being saved' and of the fact that he 'will be saved'. This is how secure the believer in Christ can be.

2. SALVATION'S CERTAINTY (verses 10 -12)

Concerning this salvation, the prophets, who spoke of the grace that was to come to you, searched intently and with the greatest care... (v. 10). Peter refers back to the prophets and shows how privileged are his readers, who have the full light of truth when compared to them. These Old Testament prophets knew they were dealing with divine truths, but that they were prophesying predominantly for future generations. But even they, though looking from a distance, searched intently so that they might understand as much as possible. Peter's readers have now experienced the wonder of God's salvation. They now have first hand knowledge of what the prophets were so intent on finding out.

The prophets, who spoke of the grace that was to come to you could be a reference to those who predicted that God's undeserved mercy would be extended to the Gentiles. In any case the essence of their message was the grace of God in Christ. Peter says that the prophets were filled with wonder at this manifestation of God's grace, and longed to know more about the Person they wrote about. They were also concerned to know when all these things were to happen.

trying to find out the time and circumstances to which the Spirit of Christ in them was pointing when he predicted the sufferings of Christ and the glories that would follow (v. 11). The 'time' was the missing link as far as the prophets were concerned. As Peter Davids comments: 'The data the prophets lacked in particular were time ("what time") and context ("what manner of time"), which were needed to give full understanding of their words, for communication has meaning only in context.'[14] The Apostle now understands that the key to unlock this is Christ.

It is clear that the prophets' message was not the result of human imagination or inspiration but rather **the Spirit of Christ in them**. This is confirmation that the Old Testament writers wrote by the Spirit of Christ. And their task, under the inspiration of the Spirit, was to testify primarily about the Person of Christ. The phrase 'Spirit of Christ' only appears on one other occasion in the New Testament (Rom. 8:9). It emphasises the fact that the Spirit in them was not only *from* Christ but that he witnessed *to* Christ.

There is no doubt that the prophets were 'inspired' by God in the full New Testament understanding of that word. Paul tells us that 'All Scripture is God-breathed' (2 Tim. 3:16) and Peter in his second letter confirms 'that no prophecy of Scripture came about by the prophet's own interpretation. For prophecy never had its origin in the will of man, but men spoke from God as they were carried along by the Holy Spirit' (2 Pet. 1:20,21). God spoke *to* them and *through* them.

There were three things in particular to which the prophets testified.

Firstly, that God's Christ, the Messiah, must suffer.

Secondly, the glories that would follow i.e. resurrection, ascension, the re-assumption of divine glory, the return of Christ, and the restitution of all things.

Thirdly, that God's saving grace would be extended towards the Gentiles.

Much of this would have been unexpected to Jews. It would have been difficult for the prophets to relate suffering with glory, and these twin aspects of truth occur more than once. For example in Isaiah 11 the prophet speaks of the Messiah coming in power and glory, and then in chapter 53 details the suffering of that Messiah. So was he to suffer or to reign? This seeming contradiction would have been a puzzle to them, yet this was the truth they had proclaimed.

The Jews were still having problems with this concept after Christ's death. When Jesus spoke to the two disciples on the road to Emmaus, he had to underline again the truth which they still had not grasped, that suffering precedes glory. Luke tells us that Jesus had to begin from Moses and the Prophets, that is the whole of the Old Testament, and explain that the Christ would have 'to suffer these things *and then* enter his glory' (Luke 24:26-27).

Even Peter himself had not been happy with the concept that his Master should suffer, until it became clear to him that this was an essential part of the Messiah's ministry. One of the 'problems' for the first century church was to explain how the Jesus who had been crucified was now Lord over all. Therefore these facts were often a focal point in their ministry (Acts 2:22-36). Peter emphasises this in his letter because he wants his readers to recognise that neither Christ nor his followers receive the crown of glory *before* the crown of thorns.

It was revealed to them that they were not serving themselves but you (v. 12). Old Testament prophets recognised that a future generation were to be the beneficiaries of their writings (See also Rom. 15:4; 1 Cor. 10:11), since **they were not serving themselves but *you*.** Though the prophets did have a message from God for the people of their own time, the Old Testament was written for the benefit of Christian believers, in order that we might understand more fully the grace of God. This fact should fill us with wonder and worship.

when they spoke of the things that have now been told you by those who have preached the gospel to you. This was the great privilege enjoyed by those of Peter's day, as well as by us today. He emphasises the fact that New Testament evangelists were now in a position to be able to understand both truths (that is suffering followed by glory) as the gospel, and preach them. They and we can now enter more fully into what was written before, yet understood in such a limited way.

This has come to them **by the Holy Spirit sent from heaven.** Jesus had told his disciples that it was necessary for him to go in order that the Spirit might come; that when Christ returns to heaven he will send the Holy Spirit to them (John 16:7) and that when he comes 'he will guide you into all truth.... He will bring glory to me by taking from what is mine and making it known to you' (John 16:13, 14).

It is the same Holy Spirit who has enabled both Old Testament prophets and New Testament apostles in their task. This is the unity of the Spirit's work in both Old and New Testaments and it should inspire great trust in the Bible as the Word of God.

Even angels long to look into these things. Peter closes this section by pointing out that even heavenly beings such as angels bend or stoop to see what God is doing here on earth. The word for 'to look into' (*parakypsai*) means literally to bow the head sideways; to look more carefully. It was used of Peter and Mary when they bent to look carefully into the tomb on the first Easter morning (John 20:5, 11). God's great work of salvation for humans produces eager interest on the part of the angels in heaven, 'since they have never known the joy that our salvation brings.'

3. SALVATION'S CHALLENGE (verses 13 -25)
These verses define God's purpose for those who enjoy salvation. First, obedience, and second holiness. That is, that we may do his will and that we might be like him.

Therefore (v. 13) – in the light of what has gone before. Salvation is something to be enjoyed by faith, but there is now an expectation from us. Having outlined the doctrine, Peter calls for a response to it. Belief should prompt behaviour. What we believe in any area of life should always dictate what we do, not least in our relationship with God.

We must act as those who mean business. Wayne Detzler affirms that 'The Church of Jesus Christ is not a dormitory for sleeping saints but rather a barrack bulging with spiritual soldiers eager to enter the battle.'[15]

So, says Peter, **prepare your minds for action**. This familiar Middle Eastern metaphor tells us to 'gird up the loins of your mind' (AV). When vigorous action was required long robes would need to be gathered up and perhaps tucked into the belt. Our equivalent might be to 'roll up your sleeves' or 'get down to it'.

Mention of the **mind** would suggest practical intelligence. It does not mean academic excellence. Hillyer remarks that 'no academic degrees are required for progress in the Christian life'.[16] The idea therefore is that we should be thoughtful about any action we take, not allowing over-enthusiasm to affect our judgment. This thoughtfulness should affect both speech and action.

be self-controlled. The Authorised Version translation 'be sober' contrasts with drunkenness which is reckless self indulgence. When an individual lets himself down because he is drunk, his friends might excuse him by saying, 'He's not himself.' In fact that is exactly what he is, because the restraints of discipline have been removed. We should be disciplined and adopt a serious attitude to what God requires as revealed in his Word. Success in many areas of life is only obtained through discipline and commitment, and a similar principle applies to the Christian life. To be 'carried away' by something and to lose our spiritual equilibrium would be in direct contradiction to this exhortation.

Peter balances his call to commitment with a reminder of their confidence: **Set your hope fully on the grace to be given you when Jesus Christ is revealed**. Whatever disciplines may be necessary for the Christian life, God's grace will be sufficient and nothing will thwart his ultimate purposes in them and for them.

As a young person I remember singing these words:

When the road is rough and steep,
Fix your eyes upon Jesus.
He alone has power to keep.
Fix your eyes upon Him.

That is what Peter is saying to these believers. Fix your eyes on the Lord, and set all your hope on him and his promised return.

This is the 'epistle of hope' and we have already noted

that hope in its fullest New Testament sense is a certain expectation. So the Christian is expected to view every aspect of his life in the light of Christ's Second Coming. The revelation of Jesus Christ at that time will bring us into the full experience of all that God has prepared for us. The promises of his grace, that is his undeserved favour wrapped up in our salvation, will be there to be enjoyed. Peter has already touched on this by referring to the inheritance (verse 4).

The fulness of God's grace is something which every Christian longs for and not least those who suffer in some specific way. In addition, to look and long for the return of Christ will strengthen us spiritually, and that in itself will inevitably bring more of the grace of God into our lives (Tit. 2:10-13).

Peter again uses the word **revealed** in connection with Christ's return not because he does not believe in Christ's presence and power being exercised at the present time but he anticipates that in that day it will be demonstrated in all its fullness.

As obedient children, do not conform to the evil desires you had when you lived in ignorance (v. 14). In verse two Peter had indicated what God had called them for: **obedience to Christ**. Now therefore, here is a title which can be rightly demanded of them: **obedient children**. This is in direct comparison to what they had been when they **lived in ignorance** (see also Eph. 2:1-3).

There is a contrast between verses 14 and 15 because becoming a Christian involves us in both the negative and the positive.

On the one hand we must not model our lives on the standards we observed when we were ignorant of the requirements of the gospel, i.e. self indulgence and the gratification of our natural appetites. It was the predictable outcome of our nature. These things cannot be properly controlled and come from a life which is ignorant of God and his law. As Wiersbe says: 'Unsaved people lack spiritual intelligence and this causes them to give themselves to all kinds of fleshly and worldly indulgences.'[17] This, therefore, should not be true of the believer.

But just as he who called you is holy, so be holy in all you do (v. 15). Here is the alternative lifestyle, the positive aspect of holiness together with the pattern to be copied; God himself. So closely are the Person and attribute woven together that grammatically this sentence could read 'like the Holy One which called you...' (RV). There is great emphasis in these words on separation *to* God.

The people of Israel, when challenged by Joshua as to who they were going to serve, casually replied, 'We will serve the Lord.' Joshua told them, 'You are not able to serve the Lord. He is a holy God.' They had not recognised the distinctiveness of the Lord, so that if they were going to link themselves in any way to him, everything about them would need to be different.

Everything associated in an intimate way with God is to be holy. This will include the Lord's Day, the Lord's house, which is the sanctuary, and God's Word, the Bible. These things are all holy because they are associated in a special way with him. So the same principle must apply to his people. God's people must be distinct and separate people. As Stuart Briscoe says: 'To be holy ... is not to be stale or sterile, but rather to be refreshingly, distinctly different.'[18]

This injunction is not an option; it is essential. It is not even an ideal to be aimed at; it is a goal to be achieved. Just as ignorance and sin are characteristics of the natural man, so obedience and holiness must be the characteristics of the spiritual man.

It is the calling which places an obligation upon us. It is, if you like, part of the requirement of being invited into membership of this exclusive society.

It should not surprise us that this kind of purity is at worst mocked and at best misunderstood outside of the church. There, the tendency is to compare your standards and lifestyle with that of others. That rule of thumb has no relevance when you belong to the family of God. God is utterly different and distinct, and this is to be the characteristic of his people. 'For those God foreknew he also predestined *to be conformed to the likeness of his Son....*' (Rom. 8:29). 'The supreme purpose of redemption is to make men holy,' says Andrew McNabb.[19]

And we are to be holy **in *all* we do**. The Christian cannot divide his life into compartments. We cannot suggest that there are areas of our lives which have nothing to do with God. *Whatever* we do is to be done to the glory of God (1 Cor. 10:31). If it cannot be done with that purpose in mind, then it should not be done at all.

for it is written: 'Be holy, because I am holy' (v. 16). This command appears a number of times in Leviticus (11:44; 20:26). It was first given to the Israelites as God's people, but now applies to the spiritual Israel, the Church of Jesus Christ. It was applied to those whom God had rescued from the bondage of slavery, and now applies to those he has rescued from the bondage of sin.

At some point in the process of our conversion there has to be a recognition of God's holiness set against our sinfulness (1 John 1:5-7). We need to be convinced of that aspect of God's nature, since it is that as much as anything which will bring the realisation of our own sinful nature. We have fallen short of God's standard (Rom. 3:23).

Following the new birth and acceptance into the family of God, holiness must be *the* characteristic of the lives of members of that family.

We repeat, this is a command; there is no question about it, since Peter confirms his own words with the words of God himself (Lev. 11:44,45; 19:2; 20:7). **It is written** was a phrase used by the Lord himself to resist Satan. Even for the devil that should have been sufficient. It must therefore be more than sufficient for us!

The answer to the question, 'Why should I be holy?', comes clearly from God – 'Because I am!' Christianity is an ethical religion, and the standard and pattern is the character of God himself. This is to be reflected throughout his family.

Since you call on a Father who judges each man's work impartially (v. 17). The term 'Father' is not used to distinguish him from the Son, but rather to state his position in the universe, and in a special way towards his children (cf. v. 14). It carries both privilege and responsibility.

Peter in the next few verses lays out some of the essentials of the gospel beginning with this truth so precious to believers. They are privileged to **call** or 'make an appeal' to the great Judge of the universe who is at one and the same time, their Father in heaven. The word translated 'call' here is the same word which Paul used when he stood trial and appealed to Caesar (Acts 25:11-12). The response was immediate. 'To Caesar you will go.' Those who call on the Father will receive an immediate audience. Peter could even have had in his mind the prayer which Jesus gave to the family of God (Matt. 6:9-13).

Stuart Briscoe says: 'We not only have a Father who is a judge, but we have a judge who is our Father.'[20] The One who judges us is the One who has brought us into his family. Wiersbe calls this 'the family judgment' between Father and children, and informs us that the word 'translated "judgeth" carries the meaning "to judge in order to find something good".'[21]

We may sometimes misunderstand God's intentions towards us, but we are reminded here that he treats all his children in a fair and just manner. The word for **impartially** is linked to the word for 'mask', so we do well to remember that when God looks at each one of us, the mask is off! Nor are we going to 'get away' with anything; God will not indulge us.

live your lives as strangers here in reverent fear. Peter reminds his readers that Christians are to live in this world as in a place to which they don't belong and where they do not expect to stay for ever. The Greek word for strangers, *paroikia,* indicates those who do not have citizenship in the country in which they live.

I have travelled extensively throughout the last thirty years and have enjoyed hospitality in many homes. I don't have any real attachment to those places, but I have always tried to be on my best behaviour when in someone else's home, and of course my own home is never far from my thoughts. The Christian has no real attachment to this earth, but for a while he lives here and has a standard to maintain, all the while keeping his mind firmly fixed on his eternal home.

The **fear** Peter speaks of is, of course, not so much a sense of being 'afraid', but rather that reverence of God which is his due even though he is our Father. The writer to the Hebrews (11:7) does tell us that 'by faith Noah, when warned about things not yet seen, *in holy fear* built an ark to save his family'. Noah was certainly fearful of the consequences of being disobedient to God! Hillyer comments on Peter's words: 'This is not the fear of cowardice or slavery, nor a self-concerned fear of death or punishment, but the proper esteem of an obedient and happy child secure in a close and warm relationship with a much admired Father.'[22] A good earthly father would expect obedience from his children, but at the same time would not want them to be afraid of him.

For you know that it was not with perishable things such as silver or gold that you were redeemed from the empty way of life handed down to you from your forefathers (v. 18). Their previous life had been 'empty' or 'vain'; words often used in relation to the worship of idols which was and is a worthless exercise because they are unable to help. It would not matter whether the readers were Jews or Gentiles the lesson would apply. For Gentiles it would have been idols, and for Jews it could have been tradition. One way or the other it was idolatry. It was vain and frivolous, says Peter.

Our redemption from that way of life, he says, was purchased with **the precious blood of Christ, a lamb without**

blemish or defect (v. 19). Redemption is a concept which would have been more quickly understood and appreciated in previous generations than now. Throughout the centuries there have been many millions of slaves, and slavery was certainly common in the Roman Empire. Slaves could be redeemed, or set free by means of a monetary payment, either from themselves or from someone else. We can only imagine the joy and relief of freedom from a life of slavery.

But our spiritual freedom could not be purchased with anything in this world, not even with silver and gold. God's redemptive work was not a business contract. No amount of money would be sufficient for this kind of redemption. It had nothing to do with anything of worldly value, and it had everything to do with the **precious** or 'highly valued' blood of Christ. This is no 'cheap' redemption of which Peter speaks. The ransom price paid was a high price indeed.

Peter is now at the heart of the gospel and speaking of Christ's sacrificial death. His perfect life, voluntarily given was the currency in this transaction. The Old Testament sacrifice involving a perfect lamb could never effectively clear the debt sinners owed to a holy God. It was a type or pattern of a perfect sacrifice to come; not an animal from another level of creation but One 'made like his brothers in every way' (Heb. 2:17). **Without blemish or defect** could be translated 'perfect outside and inside'.

The debt owed to a person depends on the price paid. God has chosen to buy us back and the price he has paid for our redemption is the death of his Son! This perfect sacrifice satisfies God's justice. Anything less would have been insufficient. Christ died the death I could not die, in order to pay the debt I could not pay.

He was chosen before the creation of the world but was revealed in these last times for your sake (v. 20). Difficult as it is to comprehend, redemption was not an afterthought. God had already planned the provision for our spiritual need before the creation of the world. Above all he knew who was going to fulfil it; his own Son, and who was going to benefit. It was **for your sake**.

In these last times indicates that the first coming of Christ was regarded as the consummation of all that God had promised and planned for redemption throughout the centuries. This verse also confirms the pre-existence of Christ in eternity past, but who has now been **revealed**.

Through him you believe in God, who raised him from the dead and glorified him, and so your faith and hope are in God (v. 21). God has laid the foundation for our faith by raising up this same Jesus and glorifying him. Peter refers back to verse 19 and the redemption provided by his death and resurrection. The reference to faith *through Christ* is a popular New Testament pattern (John 1:7; Acts 3:16; Rom. 1:8; 2 Cor. 1:20; Heb. 13:15). Christ is the catalyst in their believing. They do not only believe *in* him, they also believe *through* him.

Incidentally, this must also be of very practical encouragement for these persecuted believers. God demonstrated in Christ that he could raise the dead, so that provides good ground for their believing that he could do the same for them.

Nor was there to be the fear that belief in this message would lead people away from faith in God to faith in Jesus Christ. Rather it is through Jesus Christ that believers have been able to put their **faith and hope in God**. Peter's chequered history would keep him from any self confidence. He wanted his readers to place their faith and hope where he now has his – **in God**.

Peter now turns to the consequences of their salvation. He assumes that he is writing to believers, because he speaks of the position they are in because of their obedience to the truth of the gospel (see also verses 2 and 14): **Now that you have purified yourselves by obeying the truth so that you have sincere love for your brothers, love one another deeply, from the heart (v. 22)**.

Obeying the truth provides the contrast of the Christian message against heathen religions and their error. Yielding to that truth has been the means to purify these believers, since they now have the Holy Spirit of Christ within them.

This indwelling Spirit will also produce and reinforce that sign which Jesus said would prove their relationship with him; love for each other (John 13:35; 1 John 4:7-21; cf. John 17:23).

This is to be an indisputable badge of discipleship and an indication that a radical work of transformation has taken place. Without question there will be love for fellow Christians. 'It is impossible to love the truth and hate the brethren,' comments Wiersbe.[23]

The statement is then followed by a command that that love must be expressed **deeply, from the heart**. It is to come with full intensity, literally 'at full stretch', or in an 'all out' manner. The same word was used of Christ's praying in the Garden of Gethsemane. This will be a love that is more concerned to give than to get. That is unnatural! Natural love often has hidden motives but this 'agape' love will provide indisputable evidence that we have obeyed the truth. The Apostle John wrote, 'We know that we have passed from death to life, because we love our brothers' (1 John 3:14).

Peter's readers will be very grateful for this deep bonding when faced with persecution.

For you have been born again, not of perishable seed, but of imperishable, through the living and enduring word of God (v. 23). Peter again refers to the fact of being born again, and confirms that the instrument in this is the Word of God. He generates life through his Word and has done so from the very beginning of time (Gen. 1). Obviously the seed shares the characteristics of its Author; it is **imperishable ... and enduring**, unlike human sperm which only produces that which is corruptible.

This word from the mouth of God is life-giving truth, and when conveyed and applied to the soul, then that soul cannot die. 'He chose to give us birth through the word of truth that we might be a kind of firstfruits of all he created' (James 1:18).

Again these believers can be encouraged that the foundation they build on is quite unlike that which comes from a corruptible world. Peter quotes from Isaiah 40: 6-8 to prove his point: **For, 'All men are like grass, and all their glory is like the flowers of the field; the grass withers and the flowers fall, but the word of the Lord stands forever' (vv. 24, 25).** This chapter from the Old Testament was very popular in gospel preaching from John the Baptist onwards (John 3:31).

Everything in natural creation is transitory and frail because it is the product of perishable seed, but this is contrasted with **the word of the Lord which stands forever**. Peter applies the words from Isaiah attributed there to 'our God' to the Lord Jesus Christ. This word can never be made ineffective, and it can never be superseded. If the word is enduring, then it produces a life which is equally living and enduring so that Christians belong to a family which cannot die.

Stibbs basing his commentary on the Authorised Version text, draws attention to the fact that all that is produced from perishable seed has its day and then is described as ' "dead and gone", the exact opposite of "living and abiding".'[24]

God's word therefore offers utmost security, and says Peter, **this is the word that was preached to you**. This was the very seed that had been sown in his readers' lives through the preaching of the gospel. The word for 'preached' (*euangelizomenai*) is the word for 'to preach good news' (see Isaiah 40:9).

Could there be any better news?

References

1. Edmund P. Clowney, *The Message of 1 Peter*, IVP, 1988, p. 36.
2. Peter Davids, *I Peter*, The New International Commentary on the New Testament, Eerdmans, 1990, p. 48.
3. Michael Bentley, *Living for Christ in a Pagan World*, Evangelical Press, 1990, p. 24.
4. New Testament Commentary, Vol., 3, Cassell & Co. Ltd., 1897, p. 388.
5. Warren Wiersbe, *Be Hopeful*, Victor Books, 1982, p. 18.
6. Chuck Swindoll, *Hope Again*, Word, 1996, p. 14.
7. Stuart Briscoe, *Holy Living in a Hostile World*, Harold Shaw, 1982, p. 14.
8. N. Hillyer, *I Peter*, New International Biblical Commentary, Paternoster, 1992, p. 33.
9. A.M. Stibbs, *I Peter*, Tyndale Commentaries, 1959, p. 78.
10. Wiersbe, p. 30.
11. Wiersbe, p. 29.
12. Stibbs, p. 79.
13. Albert Barnes, Notes, Gall &Innglis, 1832, p. 152.
14. Davids, p. 61.
15. Wayne Detzler, *Living Words in 1 Peter*, Evangelical Press, 1982, p. 23.
16. Hillyer, p. 44.
17. Wiersbe, p. 40.
18. Briscoe, p. 51.
19. A. McNabb, I Peter, *The New Bible Commentary*, IVP, 1953, p. 1132.
20. Briscoe, p. 59.
21. Wiersbe, p. 43.
22. Hillyer, p. 48.
23. Wiersbe, p. 52.
24. Stibbs, p. 95.

CHAPTER TWO

THE PEOPLE OF GOD

In the first chapter Peter has laid a good foundation for the challenge he will now present. He has outlined the living hope which every believer enjoys through the new birth and the resurrection of Christ. He has emphasised the great cost to God of our salvation in a redemption purchased with the precious blood of Christ. Now he shows them the necessity of spiritual growth. Just as a new baby will only grow through healthy nourishment and the adoption of good habits, so the new Christian will need to follow a wholesome diet and a disciplined life if he is to mature. Believers facing persecution require a measure of maturity. Paul tells the Ephesians that God has provided certain gifts within the church in order that we may 'become mature, attaining to the whole measure of the fulness of Christ. *Then* we will no longer be infants, tossed back and forth by the waves, and blown here and there by every wind of teaching and by the cunning and craftiness of men in their deceitful scheming' (Eph. 4:13,14).

Spiritual growth cannot be enjoyed by sitting on the sidelines and assuming that God will do all that needs to be done. That is not his way. What God does is indispensable and miraculous, but Peter shows us that there are personal responsibilities which each believer has to fulfil.

1. THE CHRISTIAN'S DIET (verses 1-3)
A healthy life cannot be enjoyed simply by eating the right kind of food. Physical exercise must be combined with the diet to produce an all round improvement and that always requires discipline. Sadly in many quarters today the idea of discipline in any part of a person's life seems to have lost credibility. Peter however begins by suggesting an area where discipline should be exercised. There are certain characteristics which must be put aside if these believers are to progress: **Therefore rid yourselves of all malice and all deceit, hypocrisy, envy, and slander of every kind (v. 1).**

Peter is not only underlining that this should be the responsible attitude of his readers' lives, but that is a privilege

51

which they already possess. They have made a good start.
The word has been preached to them (1:25) and like good
seed in receptive soil there has been growth. They have
already been **purified ... by obeying the truth (1:22)**,
therefore the sentence could begin, '*Having* therefore ...'

The picture employed here is that of putting off dirty
clothes. It carries the idea of 'discarding'. This has sometimes
been deliberately symbolised in the sacrament of baptism,
when the candidate took off clothes before being baptised,
putting on a clean set afterwards. Though it is already true of
them in principle, the warning is still appropriate. These things
are to be cast off entirely. We are not to give any place to
them. 'Get rid of them,' says Peter. The evils mentioned here
would certainly militate against Peter's stated wish that they
should **love one another deeply, from the heart (1:22)**,
because these characteristics affect our relationships with
others.

So the list that follows is in direct contrast to what should
be the characteristics of a child of God.

The Greek word translated **malice** includes evil of all kinds
and not merely the limited usage we give to it. It is an entire
disposition to injure others without cause. The word therefore
introduces other specific evils.

Ananias and Sapphira are a good example of **deceit** (Acts
5). It can also be called guile.

Hypocrisy follows from the previous sin, that is, we
pretend to be what we are not. On more than one occasion
Jesus accused the religious leaders of his day of being
hypocrites.

Envy or jealousy means hating others because they possess
something we would like. Had Peter ever felt just a hint of
this because of the Lord's special relationship with John (John
21:20,21)?

Slander of every kind too often follows from the previous.
We run down those of whom we are jealous. Today we would
call this 'defamation of character'.

We are to rid ourselves of these sins, every one of which is an attack on our fellow man.

Twentieth century Christians need to beware of these characteristics because our old nature is very adept at them. But these features can only stunt any possible growth in our Christian lives.

Peter now demonstrates the positive. Here is the diet which will advance maturity: **Like newborn babies, crave pure spiritual milk, so that by it you may grow up in your salvation (v. 2).** There is a reference here to those who have recently been born, and it is clearly to those who have been born again by the word of God (1:23). Many of Peter's readers would be new Christians.

They are mere babies; they are immature, though in physical years some of them may be senior citizens. The Christian life needs nourishment if it is to grow strong and the diet is clearly stated: **pure spiritual milk**. This is not food for the stomach but for the soul, specifically for the spiritual life. It is logical that those born again by the word of God should feed on the 'milk of the word' (AV).

This metaphorical milk is **pure**. The word was sometimes used by merchants as a technical term for that which was unadulterated. Every member of the Christian church, and not least those who lived in the first century, needs to be fed with uncontaminated and undiluted truth. Only as each member grows, does the church as a whole grow spiritually strong, and their source of growth is 'pure milk'. This, says Peter, is the only way in which you will **grow up in your salvation**. Children will only grow properly and fully with the right kind of nutriment; the parallel is identical in the spiritual experience. Michael Bentley draws attention to the fact that the word **spiritual** is related to *logos*, the Word (Christ) and is only used in one other place in the New Testament. This is in Romans 12:1 where Paul speaks of 'spiritual ... worship.'[1]

So there is only one way to Christian maturity and that is

to **crave pure spiritual milk**. A sign of a healthy child is that he has a good appetite, and that he is ready and waiting at mealtimes. A test for spiritual health is the believer's desire for the word of God and his readiness to avail himself of every opportunity to listen to it. As Clowney states, 'Christians should be addicted to the Bible.'[2] How many Christians do I know who can't get enough of the Bible? And what about me? The word **crave** indicates how desperate should be our hunger.

In the matter of spiritual growth there is always room for improvement. Where there are limits to physical growth, there are no such limits to spiritual growth since the purpose of God is, as we have seen, that 'we should be conformed to the likeness of his Son' (Rom. 8:29). With him as the standard, all of us have a long way to go.

To be like Christ is the ultimate in Christian maturity and that points up the importance of growing up in our salvation.

now that you have tasted that the Lord is good (v. 3). 'Now' in the New International Version is better than 'if' as used in some other translations, because there is no doubt in Peter's mind that his readers have experienced the goodness of God. Usually, when 'if' is used it introduces a reason, not a query.

These believers have begun to experience the grace of God, and this should be the reason for their eagerness to know more. When we exercise taste we make a judgment and their initial experience of the truth should cause them to long for more. Not simply more of its language but more of the Lord whom they will meet in the pages of God's Word.

O send thy Spirit, Lord,
Now unto me,
That He may touch my eyes,
And make me see.
Show me the truth concealed
Within Thy Word,
And in Thy book revealed
I see the Lord.

So the milk of the word is not to be sought for its own sake, but because through it we shall come to know more of God himself. Our faith will be increased and this will bring the subsequent growth which delights the heart of God.

And what in a nutshell is the 'message' we receive? It is that **the Lord is good**. Peter quotes almost directly from the Psalmist: 'Taste and see that the LORD is good' (Ps. 34:8). Hillyer informs us that the word 'good' here 'translates the Greek *chrestos,* a play on the title Christ *(Christos).*'[3] The two words were pronounced in a similar way.

The word *chrestos* means kind, gracious and this should be the emphasis here, so perhaps our English word 'good', as we understand it today, is too general a term, as it is also in John 10:11 where the Lord is called 'the good Shepherd'.

Peter is suggesting that a mere taste of the Lord's kindness and grace toward us should be sufficient to hinder any desire to slip back into our old ways. But growth in grace through feeding on **pure spiritual milk** is the antidote to that possibility.

2. THE CHRISTIAN'S DIGNITY (verses 4-10)

Remember the context of Peter's letter. These believers were marginalised. Their self esteem would have been at rock bottom. Peter writes to confirm the status they have. By the grace of God they are members of the Church of Jesus Christ.

In a radio message R.C. Sproul asked the question, 'Who loves the Church?' He suggested that in our century it has become a monument to unbelief, and is often the centre of scandal and shame. But in answer to the question, 'Who loves the Church?' he reminded his listeners that a Christian cannot love Christ and not love the church, since it is an extension of his body. We are to recognise our identity as the people of God, and part of Christ's own body. This is the truth which Peter presses home to his readers.

As you come to him, the living Stone – rejected by men but chosen by God and precious to him (v. 4). The formation of the words 'as you come to him' (*proserchomai*) suggest a coming with the intention to stay and enjoy the relationship; in fact the verb is that which is used for coming to God in worship.

His readers had come to Christ and were now able to enjoy the privileges of the people of God. They have an access to God which for centuries had been denied them. The huge and heavy veil in the temple which separated the holiest place of all, not only presented a physical barrier, but also one that was spiritual. It told the people that God was inaccessible, until the day Christ died and it was torn like a piece of flimsy paper.

The title given to Jesus, for it is him referred to as the **living Stone**, is a reference to the basis on which the church is built (Isa. 28:16; Ps. 118:22). The foundation of the Christian Church is the prophets and the apostles, but Christ occupies the same place in regard to the church as a cornerstone does to a building. It anchors the whole building. It would not only form part of the foundation, but walls would be built from it as well as on it! So all other stones bore a relationship to it. A marvellous picture of Christ and his church.

Paul underlines this great truth in reminding the Ephesian believers of their privilege: 'You are no longer foreigners and aliens, but fellow citizens with God's people and members of God's household, built on the foundation of the apostles and prophets, with Christ Jesus himself as the chief cornerstone. In him the whole building is joined together and rises to become a holy temple in the Lord' (Eph. 2:19-21).

The word used for **stone** (*lithos*) suggests a carefully selected and hewn stone, but with no connection to either *petros* (a small rock) or *petra* (an outcrop of rock). As Detzler points out this stone 'has but one function, construction'.[4] So though our minds may make the connection between this and Peter's conversation with the Lord (Matt. 16), here Peter directs them away from himself to Christ. He would have firmly rejected any idea that they were to come to him.

And this stone is unusual because it is **living**. Usually stones are inanimate, they do not possess life; but not this one. This stone is not only a living Person but also the One who himself bestows eternal life (1 John 5:12). Peter Davids comments that this imagery designates 'Christ not as a monument or dead principle, but as the living, resurrected, and therefore life-giving one'.[5]

Two things are said about him. Firstly, he has been **rejected by men**, that is, refused as unsuitable. This could certainly be a reference to the Jewish leaders' rejection of Jesus as Messiah, but it also may have wider implications – **men**.

But in contrast he is **chosen by God and precious to him**. This is a part of the great doctrine of election. Christ is **chosen** by God. He has reversed man's verdict on Christ, who had been put to death for blasphemy. This emphasis was the central theme in the preaching of the gospel by Peter himself at Pentecost (Acts 2:22-25, 36). Indeed the builders who rejected this Stone had been sovereignly used by God to set him in place! The death and subsequent resurrection of Jesus Christ discharged the eternal purposes of God, and those who had rejected Christ had a part to play in accomplishing that plan!

So here is the contrast – **rejected by men** but **chosen by God**. Does this not have a parallel in the experience of Peter's readers? They have been rejected by men, yet Peter has emphasised that in contrast they too have been chosen by God.

The word **precious** means honoured or prized, highly esteemed. Christ is not simply a stone but a precious one. Though the word 'precious' can refer to gems, here its special relevance is to the value of the cornerstone. God has made that special selection regardless of men's valuation. So notice again that the fact that Christ was **chosen and precious** though rejected by men, emphasises God's sovereign love not only in relation to Christ, but also to those who have **come to him**. Whatever their circumstances, they can be reassured that God is in control of their situation.

Nothing in God's creation is as permanent as stones. Natural stones and especially precious stones are a wonderful visual aid of the security enjoyed by those who are **living stones**.

A popular twentieth century song informs us that 'Diamonds are forever' well almost perhaps, but not quite. They are not eternal – we are!

So, says Peter, **you also, like living stones are being built into a spiritual house to be a holy priesthood (v. 5)**. 'Living' is better than 'lively' (AV). All the materials in this building are 'living', being made spiritually alive by the resurrection life of the Cornerstone, and together they are **being built into a spiritual house**. This is a beautiful description of the purpose of the church. Many people have a variety of ideas as to why the church exists. Most sum it up in the phrase 'Hatch, match and dispatch', that is to christen, marry and bury. Scripture has loftier ideas than that. It shows us that it is not only *a bride to be something* (Rev. 19:7,8) and *a body to do something* (Rom. 12:4,5) but here fundamentally, it is *a building for the pleasure of God.*

Stibbs links this description of Peter's with his confession of Christ in Matthew 16. He suggests that Jesus was saying there, 'Now you are a stone and I want many similar stones, because I intend with them to build a church; and to build it upon, or in relation to Myself thus confessed as Christ, as the basic Rock, the unifying chief cornerstone.'[6]

The background is of course the symbolism of the Old Testament where the temple was understood to be the dwelling place of God. But that temple was built with inanimate stones. Here is a situation where the spiritual church replaces the material temple in Jerusalem. Jesus spoke along these lines when he conversed with the woman of Samaria (John 4:21,23-24).

This building, made up of living stones, is to be a temple where God by his Holy Spirit indwells his people. It is a

spiritual house with a priesthood and the offering of sacrifices.
The Old Testament priesthood was restricted to the tribe of
Levi because of their loyalty in connection with the golden
calf idolatry (Exod. 32:26). Now in the new covenant the
priesthood is a privilege open to all in Christ. In a peculiar
way no one is to be a priest because the priest offered a
physical sacrifice which is no longer required, yet everyone
is a priest because now we are **offering spiritual sacrifices**.
The idea of priesthood attached to New Testament believers
may also include the thought of those who have separated to
God (Lev. 8–11).

In the Old Testament it was not always known if an animal
sacrifice would be accepted (Heb. 10:1-10), but spiritual
sacrifices are **acceptable to God**, because obedience and
holiness were something that animal sacrifices could not
bring. Above all, these new sacrifices are acceptable because
they are offered **through Jesus Christ**, and not because of
the merit of the person who is making the offering. This is a
salutary reminder that whatever we do for God is dependant
on the work of Christ for its acceptability.

In verses 6-8 Peter uses three Old Testament passages to
show that the position which Christ occupies as the chief
cornerstone was foreordained by God. He also contrasts the
different responses that the same stone can prompt.

The first quotation is taken from Isaiah 28:16: **For in
Scripture it says: 'See, I lay a stone in Zion, a chosen and
precious cornerstone, and the one who trusts in him will
never be put to shame' (v. 6)**. These words were treated as
Messianic, and so directly related to Jesus Christ. The Zion
referred to is the heavenly or spiritual Jerusalem. The stone
laid by God himself is the cornerstone which was that
specially selected stone which was worked on and squared
off to fulfil its purpose, and those trusting in him 'will not
find their confidence misplaced' is what the final words mean.

Now to you who believe, this stone is precious (v. 7).
The popular understanding of this phrase is that the One who

was precious to God (v. 4), the only begotten, who always pleased his Father has now become precious to those who believe. However Hillyer points out that this is not what the Greek means. 'The Greek says nothing about "this stone" here, but runs .... literally "to you believers (is) the honour." This balances the thought of the dishonour that Peter indicates in this passage is the lot of unbelievers. Why should translators shy away from suggesting that the people of God are to be honoured?... To be sure the honour is due not to any individual's status, worthiness, or achievements, but it is solely the consequence of being made a member of God's family through Jesus Christ. That is the glorious prospect of you who believe.'[7]

If the words are to be understood in this way then they link with the 'praise, glory and honour' of 1:7.

The second quotation is from Psalm 118:22: **But to those who do not believe, 'The stone which the builders rejected has become the capstone.'** This is a reference to the same stone as before; the chief cornerstone or 'the head of the corner'. Builders would examine stones before starting to build and some would be rejected or literally 'disapproved' or 'disallowed'. The 'builders' rejecting this 'stone' were the religious leaders, but God has taken that Stone and made it the central unifying stone of the temple. Peter had used this quotation before when preaching before the Sanhedrin (Acts 4:7-11).

The third quotation from the Old Testament is from Isaiah 8:14: **and 'A stone that causes men to stumble and a rock that makes them fall' (v. 8)**. Still a stone, but now a stumbling stone. This 'capstone' is not necessarily on top, but rather as before, the stone on the ground; the cornerstone over which men might trip, or a rock in the road which might cause them to fall. This is what the person and work of Christ is **to those who do not believe**. Men and women must meet this 'Stone' since he is placed in their path; the manner of their encounter is determined by their faith or otherwise. This stone places a divide between believers and unbelievers.

Peter surely remembered that Jesus had applied the same word for 'stumbling block' to him when he had tried to deflect Christ from the cross. 'You are a stumbling block to me; you do not have in mind the things of God, but the things of men' (Matt. 16:23). And this was just after his clear declaration as to Christ's person. 'You are the Christ, the Son of the living God' (v. 16).

And why do they stumble? **Because they disobey the message.** The essential problem is not a lack of understanding, but rather disobedience to the word of God.

When Jesus explained to his disciples why he had changed his teaching method by speaking to the people in parables, he said it was because of a wilful rejection by some who, though they had received increasing evidence of who he was, refused to believe. For them it was primarily a case of 'would not' believe rather than 'could not' believe (Matt. 13).

The disposition of some today towards Christ is no different. To these he is a stumbling block. The One who could be for them is against them. But, says Peter, this is not an issue of chance. It is **what they were destined for**. It was never thought that all would embrace Christ, and there is certainly an indication in these words that there is an initiative behind it, so that both God's sovereignty and human responsibility are present here.

They are condemned because they **do not believe** and this disobedience is within the Sovereign will of God (Rom. 9:14-24). They were **destined** or appointed, and the end result is in conformity with that. The Greek word used for 'destined' is the same as the word used for 'lay' as in a builder laying a foundation, settling it into its place. So God settles man's choice. This is God's appointed outworking of judgment on unbelief.

But you are a chosen people (v. 9). Here is the wonderful contrast. **But you**, says Peter, expect an entirely different prospect. These believers, indeed all believers are **a chosen**

people or an elect race. The same word is used in 1:1. The new birth in 1:23 has brought them into a new family; they are a 'people'. Each of the privileges of believers which Peter mentions in this verse emphasises the unity they enjoy. As Michael Bentley points out, 'Peter says, "You need to be reminded of what you are. You are not a hotchpotch of individuals. You are a people, a nation. You are a collection of God's people. You have been brought together to stand together and to live for God together." '[8]

Great Britain is made up of many individuals but when, for example, it is said, '*The people* of Great Britain speak', it suggests a sublimating of their individuality to express the united view of the whole. So when God calls individuals to himself (Acts 16:14), that does not permit them to 'do their own thing'; by definition they become part of 'a people' with both privileges and responsibilities to God, and to each other. Bentley again, 'God does not use bricks in his building. Bricks all tend to be made in the same way. They all have the same dimensions. They all look the same. When God planned his church he decided to use individual stones for it. These have all been hand-picked by him. They are all shaped individually to fit into the exact place in his house for which they have been chosen.'[9]

The fact that a divine choice has been made is at the heart of the gospel, and yet it is so often a subject of controversy amongst believers. The wonder of salvation is not that God chose some against others, but that he chose any at all! As Clowney points out: 'Certainly God does not choose an elite. Israel is a chosen people but not a choice people. God's elect have no ground for pride.'[10]

Paul shows us that God chooses anything but good material (1 Cor. 1:29). So what motivates his choice? The answer for the old and new Israel is the sovereign love of God (Deut. 7:7f.). God's love for the sinner defies explanation.

But they are also **a royal priesthood**. They bear the dignity of kings and the sanctity of priests. Because of their position in Christ, they belong not to any earthly kingdom, but to the kingdom of God; they are indeed 'royal'. As priests they have 'the privilege of serving in the presence of the deity, of coming near when no one else dares (cf. Heb. 9:1–10:25). Thus together, the words indicate the privileged position of Christians before God: belonging to the king and in the presence of God.'[11]

They have been called to reign and serve. Jesus Christ 'has made us a kingdom and priests to serve his God and Father' (Rev 1:6).

And they are **a holy nation**. The Jews were considered a nation consecrated to God i.e. holy. 'Although the whole earth is mine, you will be for me a kingdom of priests *and a holy nation*' (Exod. 19:5,6). This language is now applied to the people God has chosen in a similar way; the Christian church, the only group in society thus described. Notice again the corporate identity of the people of God.

But important though it is to be separated to God, we are not to be isolated from the world. It is, as Wiersbe says, 'contact without contamination'. Jesus told us that we are to remain here as salt and light in order that the world 'may see your good deeds and praise your Father in heaven' (Matt. 5:16).

Then for their great encouragement, Peter tells them that they are **a people belonging to God**. This translates 'a peculiar people' (AV). The word 'peculiar' in the King James Version is the translation of a 'special, highly valued property'. Something which was a person's very own possession. It was used for instance, of the personal treasure of a king as distinct from the nation's wealth. So believers are a people who are God's precious possession; a wonderful assurance to Peter's readers.

Stuart Briscoe illustrates the thought beautifully when he remembers that as a child he used to sing the chorus, 'When he cometh, when he cometh to make up his jewels.' (I too remember it well!) He asked his mother, 'Mother, who are Jesus' jewels?' She replied, 'You are.' So for a while he says

he strutted around like a jewel. Then he forgot all about it.
Years later he was reading Malachi 3:17 (AV): 'They will be
mine... when I make up my jewels,' and he realised that the
hymn writer got his idea from Malachi. And so did Peter,
because the word Peter uses is the same as is used in the
Greek translation of Malachi 3:17.[12]

Peter informs them that they enjoy these privileges **that
you may declare the praises of him who called you out of
darkness into his wonderful light**. To **declare the praises**
is to show the excellence or good qualities. To proclaim to
those without, what has taken place within. This elevates the
worship and praise in our church services to its rightful place.
As Clowney says: 'If the singing and speaking forth of the
praises of God are viewed as "preliminaries" to the sermon,
the meaning of worship has been lost.'[13]

The verse closes with a common New Testament
expression describing the change brought about by the gospel
on the unbeliever. Again the divine initiative is emphasised.
It is of **him who called you**. We have received a royal
invitation to be part of 'a people'. Our nature was characterised by **darkness** which would lead to destruction and death.
But praise be to God, he has 'qualified (us) to share in the
inheritance of the saints in the kingdom of light. For he has
rescued us from the dominion of darkness and brought us
into the kingdom of the Son he loves' (Col. 1:12,13). We
have every reason therefore to declare his praises.

**Once you were not a people, but now you are the people
of God (v. 10)**. Peter uses the language of Hosea 2:23: 'I will
say to those called "Not my people," "You are my people"
and they will say "You are my God".' The background of
Hosea is that of an unfaithful wife restored to her husband.
How does that prophecy relate to Peter's readers? If 'the
people of God' was a phrase reserved for Israel in the Old
Testament, then 'not my people' must refer to Gentiles. So
Gentiles who previously had not featured in God's plan, now
become part of the elect people of God. He says to them now,

'You *are* my people' and as such they look forward to a glorious destiny. Paul uses the same verses in a similar way (Rom. 9:25-26).

Equally **once you had not received mercy, but now you have received mercy**. Again the words come from Hosea. Those in Scripture who cried out for mercy from God, or God's Son were never turned away. He took pity on them and gave them what they did not deserve.

A widow once appealed to Napoleon for mercy for her son after he had fallen foul of the Emperor through some misdeed. Napoleon replied that her son did not deserve mercy. 'If he deserved it, it would not be mercy, and mercy is what I ask,' said the widow.

Once these believers, and we too, lived in ignorance, without pardon and without knowledge of the way sins could be forgiven; **but now**: the tense used indicates a decisive moment when through the hearing, and understanding, and obedience to the gospel, this change was brought about.

3. THE CHRISTIAN'S DUTY (verses 11-25)

The privileged position which a believer now enjoys, places some demands upon him. He has been '*ransomed*, healed, restored, forgiven'. He is 'free', but not free from respons-ibility. The world regards 'freedom' as the liberty for each person to do exactly as he or she wishes without any outward restraint. In practice this is of course a nonsense, and a totally false proposition. The keys I carry in my pocket are evidence that I cannot trust my fellow man, because I need to secure my property lest his view of 'freedom' is different to mine and permits him to steal it. Our lives are put in danger every day because there are those who object to being subject to road traffic laws. Traditional laws and values are overturned at will because we are told man has the right to be 'free'. It is fast becoming a world without absolutes of any kind.

These examples illustrate the foolishness of liberty as defined by the world. Simply stated, liberty is not freedom to do as you want. In contrast, the believer who is truly free has different standards. He is a slave of Jesus Christ, and is also required to be a servant to his fellow man, and that in biblical terms, is liberty. True freedom is best enjoyed within the parameters which God has provided, and in which we love and obey God and love and serve our fellowmen. Liberty is therefore not freedom to live as I want, but rather freedom to live as I ought. Peter deals with some of the practical outworking of this in the following section.

Dear friends, I urge you, as aliens and strangers in the world, to abstain from sinful desires, which war against your soul (v. 11). In this verse we have the negative, and the next contains the positive. As members of the people of God, we are by definition **strangers** to the rest of society. The words **aliens** and **strangers** indicate detachment from the world. If you are only a temporary resident in a country, you are not expected to slavishly follow all the local customs. So Peter emphasises that it will have value to us as those who are transients here, to act in a disciplined way, and to distance ourselves from some of the characteristics and customs of the world.

The real battle of course is not from *without* but from *within.* Wiersbe quotes D L Moody as saying, 'I have more trouble with D L Moody than with any man I know.'[14] Indiscipline in our own personal lives will serve to **war against the soul**. 'War' here implies not just one battle but many.

What of those occasions when our professed faith does not mean to us all we expect or desire? What of those times when spiritual things have, quite frankly, lost their sparkle? The hymn writer knew such an experience:

Where is the blessedness I knew
When first I saw the Lord?
Where is the soul refreshing view
Of Jesus and His word?

The reason could be that we have given way to **sinful desires**. To the believer, they are like caged yet wild animals. To avoid even the possibility of danger they must not be give the merest 'sniff' of freedom. We need God's strength and the support of his people to do this.

The contrast that Peter paints here is between satisfying the sinful desires of the 'flesh' which is part of the old life, and the well-being of the 'soul' which is made for eternity.

But we have already noticed that Christians are not to be isolationists. In the next verse he underlines that they **live ... among the pagans**. We may be *in* the world but we are not to be *of* the world, and there is a very good reason for that.

Says Peter, **Live such good lives among the pagans that, though they accuse you of doing wrong, they may see your good deeds and glorify God on the day he visits us (v. 12)**. Here then is the positive action we must take. There is no mistaking *where* we live – **among the pagans** – and there should be no misunderstanding as to *how* we live. In direct contrast to the pagans, we are to live **good lives**. The quality of our lives should be such that ultimately they will point away from ourselves to God. Men will see that the beauty and attractiveness which characterises the believer's life is only possible through some outside agency.

The theologians refer to God's common grace bestowed on all, in contrast to God's special grace shown toward certain individuals. Much of God's common grace has been mediated through the church. Such major social changes as the abolition of the slave trade, the hospital movement, the education system, orphanages and much more have been driven by Christian thinkers. R C Sproul refers to this as the legacy of the church to the welfare of our nations. This is living out the Christian ethic before the world.

There will always be the possibility of false accusation and Christ himself is the perfect illustration of this. The perverseness of human nature will still attribute wrong and unworthy motives to our words and actions. The Roman

historian Tacitus tells us that Christians were 'loathed because
of their abominations'. First century Christians were charged
with immorality because of their emphasis on 'love'. They
were even accused of cannibalism because it was heard that
they ate flesh and drank blood at their special feasts! All of
this is best answered by deeds not words, notwithstanding
the consequences. For many in Peter's day, including himself,
it would mean death.

Our conduct must be such as will bear the closest scrutiny,
so that even when we are carefully examined, honesty and
uprightness will be found.

The day referred to, is generally considered to be any day
of crisis, as for instance when God brings a man to repentance
and faith. It is probably to be regarded as a day which brings
favour rather than judgment. The attitude of some will be
changed as they see the obedience of believers and that will
glorify God (See also Rev. 11:13). Peter illustrates this later,
when he refers to unbelieving husbands being won to Christ
through the behaviour of their believing wives (3:1,2).

Now Peter illustrates a further outworking of Christian
doctrine in the next verse: **Submit yourselves for the Lord's
sake to every authority instituted among men (v. 13)**. Sin,
the characteristic of unbelief, is an act of rebellion, and as
such is disobedience to the law of God. It is epitomised in
the man of lawlessness because of his defiance against God
(2 Thess. 2:3). Since it is God himself who delegates authority
to earthly powers, Christians must be model citizens in their
submission to those authorities. Rebellion is not part of the
scenario.

The submission of which Peter now begins to speak covers
a variety of relationships. In these verses it is our submission
to those entrusted with the power of government. Then later,
slaves to masters (v. 18f.), wives to husbands (3:1f.), in a
different sense husbands to wives (3:7) and finally, believers
to each other (3:8f.).

The literal meaning in the first of these (2:13) suggests

'every creation of man' but our submission **to every authority instituted among men** is only to the extent that that authority is not acting contrary to the law of God. Our primary obedience is always to God. We are to submit to every authority that is placed over us in this world except when that authority commands us to do something which God forbids, or forbids us to do something which God commands.

The Hebrew midwives were right to refuse to obey Pharaoh when he told them to kill all new born Hebrew boys, because 'they feared God.' (Exod. 1:17). When forbidden to speak in the name of Christ, the apostles were right when they said to the Sanhedrin, 'We must obey God rather than men!' (Acts 5:29). So the same man who was to write, 'Submit yourselves to every authority', said 'No' on that occasion to authority. In many situations the influence of the state extends into a variety of areas which in unsympathetic circumstances will inevitably lead to conflict with the church. If the church owes its ultimate allegiance to God, and if the state does not, they are on a collision course. In Acts 5:29 Peter uses what Briscoe calls a 'simple escape clause', under the only condition in which this is permitted. The principle is easy to articulate and easy to understand, but not always so easy to apply.

Acknowledging the escape clause, there is to be respect and honour for earthly powers. Christians can have no truck with anarchy. I must drive within the speed limit, and I must pay the taxes which the state demands. The God we profess to trust is a God of order, and to maintain the order of society we must follow the rules. As Sproul says: 'Believers are to maintain the order of the universe when others engage in radical individualism.'

Peter's command here complements Paul's exhortation to the Romans. 'Everyone must submit himself to the governing authorities for there is no authority except that which God has established' (13:1). Paul makes clear that a government's ultimate authority comes from God and to reject that delegated authority is to reject God's authority. In

Proverbs 8:15 God reminds us, 'By me kings reign and rulers make laws that are just.'

Peter underlines the motivation: **for the Lord's sake**. We could understand submitting to the authority of God for the Lord's sake, but here we are to submit to the ordinances of man 'for the Lord's sake.' This of course covers everything that the believer does but in this special case because we are the Lord's representatives.

Stibbs suggests three possible interpretations of this phrase. Because

(1) Christians recognise such institutions as divinely ordained, therefore their submission is to the Lord.

(2) The Lord himself was submissive and we should follow his example.

(3) That we might commend Christ as Lord to others, and not bring reproach on his name.[15]

Certainly this is something a Christian should choose to do, rather than be compelled to do. The believer recognises that the one in a position of authority is due respect, firstly, because of the fact that he is a creature of God, and secondly, we honour him because he has been entrusted with this stewardship of responsibility by God himself. Obedience to authority is therefore ultimately fulfilling the purposes of God. The fact that part of his plan includes sinners, means that sometimes the authorities misuse their power but this does not give us the right to reject their authority. Our Lord understood this truth when he stood before Pilate. The Roman governor had said that he had power to free him or to crucify him, but Jesus replied 'You would have no power over me *if it were not given to you from above*' (John 19:10,11).

Then follows a list of these authorities.

whether to the king, as the supreme authority. Surely in Peter's mind would be particular reference to Roman emperors, but includes any in whom rests supreme authority. There is no word for 'emperor' in Greek so the word for 'king' is substituted (as also in verse 17). This may seem a straightforward instruction to us, but was to have a special relevance to Christians in that century. The rough treatment they were to face invariably emanated from the emperor.

or to governors, who are sent by him to punish those who do wrong, and to commend those who do right (v. 14). Governors were subordinate officers in charge of an area and answerable to the supreme authority, and the 'him' who sends is almost certainly the emperor, rather than God.

They punish evil doers and commend or praise those who do right. In other words ideally they are concerned with the promotion of moral behaviour. That is to be commended and supported by Christians.

For it is God's will that by doing good you should silence the ignorant talk of foolish men (v. 15). Doing good will **silence** or 'muzzle', says Peter. It is a contemptuous term which almost suggests the animal in their accusers, whose **ignorant talk** is more than a lack of knowledge, but rather an unwillingness to accept the truth. Those who criticise a life of absolute integrity are **foolish men**; those without reason, senseless. When the Bible uses the word 'foolish', it implies the leaving of God out of the equation (Ps. 14:1; Luke 12:20), and that is exactly what these people are doing when they make false accusations against Christians.

Live as free men, but do not use your freedom as a cover-up for evil; live as servants of God (v. 16). Peter's readers were to regard themselves as free men with the right to liberty, but showing that their true liberty was to be servants of God. A man is a dependent being and the truest liberty he can experience is to make all his faculties available to the service of God. Nothing else provides true freedom, which is what Jesus was offering during his time on earth (John 8:32). It is a wonderful paradox: **Live as free men ... live as servants** (bond slaves) **of God**. To voluntarily serve others in the name of Christ and for no other motive, puts a question mark in the mind of the pagan. It is contrary to the attitude of the world which often has an ulterior and selfish motive.

The Christian should never abuse his liberty or use it as a **cover-up for evil**, or as 'a curtain for vice' (AV). The man Peter is thinking of is not guilty of simple hypocrisy because he is not professing to be better than he is. He loudly asserts that he is not a slave, and men admire such freedom of speech, and excuse his vices because he is so open about them.

We are only free because Christ has made us so, and at great cost. That places on us an obligation toward the One who bought us. Barclay makes the point clear: 'Christian freedom does not mean being free to do as we like; it means being free to do as we ought.'[16] We therefore use our freedom for others and not for ourselves.

The next verse is a comprehensive catechism.

Show proper respect to everyone (v. 17). This emphasises the truth running through all these verses that to show respect for everyone is the right attitude and is to be commended. The believer may rejoice in his position before God, but he will never be able to attribute it to something he was or did which elevates him above his fellow man. Only the grace of God has made him what he is.

Love the brotherhood of believers. These words suggest more than love for our individual brother in Christ, but rather to love the community of believers i.e. the church. It is easy, even popular, to criticise the church because it is made up of fallible sinners, but the church means a great deal to Christ. Paul told the Ephesian elders to 'be shepherds of *the church of God, which he bought with his own blood*' (Acts 20:28).

fear God. As honour is due to all men as creatures of God, so reverence is due to God himself. The pagan does not honour God with the respect that his creatorship and majesty deserve. Yet without him we are nothing, and have nothing. The believer acknowledges this, and so should set the tone in society. To **fear God** will of course include implicit obedience. We have already drawn attention to this in the life of Noah (Heb. 11:7). This is what it means to be spiritual in a secular world.

honour the king. This is the point at which some of Peter's readers would have real difficulty. For them the Roman emperor would be the symbol of all that was set against them. But whether the ruler is good, bad, or indifferent, he is to be accorded respect because he has been ordained by God. It is interesting to note that the word for 'honour' *(timan)* is the same as is translated previously by 'show proper respect' so is Peter also implying that though a Roman emperor expected to be treated like a god, he was essentially no different to anyone else?

So Peter takes them through their catechism: Show all men respect, love the brethren, fear God and honour the king, and the tense of the words shows us that they are to 'keep on' doing these things.

The principle of submission continues as Peter deals with relationships between slaves and masters: **Slaves, submit yourselves to your masters with all respect, not only to those who are good and considerate, but also to those who are harsh (v. 18).**

There were many slaves in the first century, though the situation was changing. Nowhere does the New Testament encourage slaves to revolt, nor does it suggest that Christian masters should allow their servants to go. The New Testament does not agree with slavery, but in their current circumstances it emphasises the importance of respect from both sides.

Peter does not use the usual word for 'slaves' in the New Testament *(douloi)*, but the one that refers to domestics, *oiketai*. The reference here is therefore to the household, and many of these servants would have responsible positions. That would include areas of employment which we might describe today as 'professional', e.g. doctors, estate managers and teachers. These servants therefore had a settled place in society but of course they were not free, though some might eventually have the means to purchase their own freedom.

The problem with Christian slaves was that some masters might feel their position threatened by a servant who professed a higher allegiance to another Master. This would inevitably mean a variety of pressures on that servant.

Masters, says Peter are of two kinds: **good and considerate** and **harsh**. Some are fair and reasonable, others will be 'bent' or 'crooked' is the literal meaning. They may be unfair and awkward to deal with. You don't know what they are going to do next. How should the Christian slave react in that kind of situation? He must follow the principle of submission regardless of what kind of master he has – and it is to be done with **respect**. Employees are in a very similar situation today, and those who are Christians should follow the same principles.

For it is commendable if a man bears up under the pain of unjust suffering because he is conscious of God (v. 19). The word translated 'commendable' both here and in verse 20 is the word *charis,* meaning 'grace' or 'gracious'. To bear up in that situation would be pleasing to God because it is an expression of grace and evidence of the change which he has brought about. It illustrates true spiritual freedom, which does not require payment of evil for evil. If I respond in kind, which would be perfectly natural, then I confirm that I am a slave – in bondage. If I can bear the injustice patiently, I break the chain of slavery and show that I am confident of God's justice.

The slave who is a believer will act in this way because he is God's slave and cannot therefore be a slave to his earthly master. His daily service is performed ultimately for the Lord, and he respects his master (v. 18) for the Lord's sake. What this slave does, he does willingly, and who can tell what a good influence this might have on his earthly master.

But how is it to your credit if you receive a beating for doing wrong and endure it? But if you suffer for doing good and you endure it, this is commendable before God (v. 20). There is to be no praise for being dealt with harshly if you deserve it, even if you accept it patiently. Inefficient work or a rebellious attitude deserves punishment not reward. But unjust punishment will provide an opportunity for that servant to show evidence of the grace of God in his life.

They must accept that this is to be expected by the very nature of their Christian faith. **To this you were called (v. 21)**. The combination of suffering for well doing is a characteristic of Christianity. Paul often warned of it (e.g. 1 Thess. 3:3,4).

Clowney contrasts the glory of God's calling with the suffering they are experiencing: 'Christians have been called out of darkness into God's marvellous light (2:9). They are called as God's elect, his chosen people, heirs of his blessing (3:9). But now Peter says, *To this you were called.* To what? To suffering, to unjust abuse, to patient endurance when they are beaten for doing right! Peter has described our heavenly calling; he does not conceal our earthly calling.'[17]

This 'calling' is of course not unique to these first century Christians to whom Peter is writing. It is to be the calling of all who profess Christ. Paul makes that point when he writes to Timothy. He speaks of his own sufferings, pays tribute that 'the Lord rescued me from all of them' and then confirms, 'Everyone who wants to live a godly life in Christ Jesus will be persecuted' (2 Tim. 2:13). Believers in every generation have proved this – including our own. It is said that more Christians have been martyred in the twentieth century than in all other centuries put together.

Now follows the justification for this **because Christ suffered for you, leaving you an example**. Is there any reason why the servant should be above his Master?

There are three main aspects to his example:

(1) Christ suffered because he was the Christ.

(2) His suffering was for others, not on his own account – **for you**.

(3) We would also suffer, and we have our example in him.

Peter rebelled against these ideas when Jesus spoke to him as a disciple, but here he shows how fully he has understood and accepted them. Jesus Christ is a perfect example of

suffering for well doing. But then we might suggest that he is
not unique in that. There are others who are examples of this
in their own way. The extra dimension that is in Peter's mind
is referred to later when he speaks of Christ's atonement,
which included the purpose that we might **die to sins and
live for righteousness (v. 24)**. That is the ultimate reason
why we should mark his example and **follow in his steps**.
Peter no doubt remembers his own failures brought about
because he was not 'following' his Lord closely enough. Here
he encourages his readers to follow so closely
(*epakolouthein*), as to step into his foot marks (*ichnesin*).

Peter had been as close to Jesus as anyone, and by quoting
Isaiah 53:9, he adds his own confirmation of Christ's
sinlessness: **He committed no sin, and no deceit was found
in his mouth (v. 22)**. It is appropriate that this passage in
Isaiah speaks of the suffering Servant.

These two phrases cover every aspect of his life, in deed
and word. They not only confirm his sinlessness, but for the
benefit of these first century believers also underline the fact
that he did not *deserve* to suffer, and in that he is the perfect
example of suffering for **doing good (v. 20)**.

**When they hurled insults at him, he did not retaliate;
when he suffered, he made no threats. Instead he entrusted
himself to him who judges justly (v. 23).** How does Peter
know these things? He tells us later that he was **a witness of
Christ's sufferings (5:1)**.

Peter remembered when they spoke of Jesus being a
deceiver, in league with the devil, a blasphemer, that Christ
used no harsh language in return. He called for no revenge.
When he suffered injustice from others he did not call down
the wrath of heaven on them.

But this was not simply a negative silence – there was a
positive response – **he entrusted himself to him who judges
justly.** He committed his case to God. Though wronged by
men in so many ways, he knew that God would be just. For
believers this is 'the bottom line.' We can confidently leave

all of this with the One who is 'taking it all in' and who has the ultimate responsibility to dispense justice.

Jesus also realised the purpose behind his suffering. It concerned the justice of God. In letting shame and suffering heap itself on him, the righteous God was judging righteously.

In suffering injustice, Christ was dealing with sin. When we recognise injustice for what it is, a characteristic of sin, it changes our view of those who act unjustly toward us. We do not simply regard them as unkind, unfair or cruel, which would be the world's view and would encourage retaliation. We see them as sinners for whom we are to have compassion. This is the Christian (the Christlike) way of handling injustice.

But Christ did not only suffer insults and threats. Peter tells us that he died an ignominious death: **He himself bore our sins in his body on the tree, so that we might die to sins and live for righteousness; by his wounds you have been healed (v. 24)**. Peter is continuing to 'quote' from Isaiah 53 though not directly. So taken up is he with that passage that many of the thoughts in the remainder of this chapter reflect the language of those verses.

Peter underlines two facts. First, he stressed that Christ died for sins, and second, they were not his own. His death was penal, and yet it was substitutionary, since he has already said that it was **'for you'** (v. 21). Peter sensitively and gladly now includes himself: **he himself bore *our* sins**.

He specifically refers to Christ's death **on the tree**. The Jews were insistent that he should be crucified to heap upon him the maximum shame (Gal. 3:13). Crucifixion was a Roman practice and not the normal form of execution for a Jew. A Jew after stoning was hung on a tree as symbol of shame for a particularly heinous offence (Deut. 21:23).

To make direct reference to 'tree' was familiar language for Peter (Acts 5:30; 10:39) and, as Hillyer points out, 'For a reader familiar with the Old Testament background, "to be hanged on a tree" is more meaningful than "to be crucified," for the implication of the former expression is that by dying in that manner Jesus bears the punishment for all who break the divine law.'[18] (See again Gal. 3:13.)

The purpose behind Christ's death was to bring separation between men and their sins and to reconcile those individuals to God. Sin had brought separation between God and man. Now Christ removes that barrier and makes provision for another separation to take place between man and his sin. This sacrifice deals with every aspect of sin. The guilt of the past is cancelled, its power in the present is dethroned and ultimately its very presence in our lives will be removed.

The word used for **die** here in reference to the believer and his relationship with sin, is only used on this one occasion in the New Testament and it emphasises this idea of separation. To **die to sins** means literally 'to be missing – to be away from'. When sin comes to seek its old servants it finds them gone! The purpose of his death was to enable us to live a life henceforth that is pleasing to God.

The reference to healing here is primarily a reference to spiritual healing, though this verse as found in Isaiah (53:5), is also applied to our Lord's healing ministry in the gospels (Matt. 8:17).

Stibbs points out: 'paradoxically, it is through the hurt done to Him, that they get healing'.[19] The slave would be familiar with the bruise left by the lash, so the Son of God has borne the same and they have benefited.

This next verse confirms that spiritual healing was what his readers needed: **For you were like sheep going astray, but now you have returned to the Shepherd and Overseer of your souls (v. 25).** Peter is still in Isaiah 53, with verse 6 in mind. The sheep/shepherd imagery is familiar language both in the Old and New Testaments. Many of the writers used the roaming of sheep as a picture of the purposeless wandering of lost mankind. But now things are different: **You were ... but now.** There has been a turning around – a conversion. The aimless wandering has finished, just as a sheep's wandering ends when it is linked up to the shepherd.

Now there is direction and purpose. How true this had been for Peter himself. 'When you have *turned back*, strengthen your brothers' (Luke 22:32) was his Lord's instruction.

Overseer describes the Shepherd, rather than being a separate title. Peter is speaking of the overseeing Shepherd; the One who exercises pastoral care and oversight with particular concern for **our souls**. It means that the soul committed to him could not be in better hands. Peter tells his readers and us, that the world will be looking *at* us, so we must live godly lives, but there is also One in heaven who is looking *over* us and that provides a wonderful assurance.

References

1. M. Bentley, *Living for Christ in a Pagan World*, Evangelical Press, 1990, p. 66.
2. Edmund P Clowney, *The Message of 1 Peter*, IVP, 1988, p. 78.
3. Hillyer, *I Peter*, New International Biblical Commentary, Paternoster, 1992, p. 57.
4. Wayne Detzler, *Living Words in 1 Peter*, Evangelical Press, 1982, p. 35.
5. Peter Davids, *I Peter*, The New International Commentary on the New Testament, Eerdmans, 1990, p. 85.
6. A. M. Stibbs, *I Peter*, Tyndale Commentaries, 1959, p. 99.
7. Hillyer, p. 63.
8. Bentley, p. 76.
9. Bentley, p. 77.
10. Clowney, p. 91.
11. Davids, p. 92.
12. Stuart Briscoe, *Holy Living in a Hostile World*, Harold Shaw, 1982, p. 88.
13. Clowney, p. 96.
14. Warren Wiersbe, *Be Hopeful*, Victor, 1982, p. 63.
15. Stibbs, p. 110.
16. William Barclay, *The Letters of James and Peter*, DSB, 1975, p. 207.
17. Clowney, p. 116.
18. Hillyer, p. 86.
19. Stibbs, p. 121.

CHAPTER
THREE

SUBMISSION,
SYMPATHY
AND
SUFFERING

Peter continues a similar theme but with the emphasis now on family relationships.

1. SUBMISSION (verses 1-7)

He begins by addressing Christian wives. Our generation is one where so-called 'political correctness' and its various expressions is a hot potato. Society is obsessed with sexual equality and the swings and roundabouts have determined that we should live at a time when feminism is a powerful force.

Peter would surely be 'considered outmoded, if not treacherous for suggesting that men and women have different roles.... Peter was impetuous enough to swing a sword at officers arresting Jesus. He also debated fearlessly with a daunting spokesman like Paul. One doubts that he would shrink from speaking out on the subject of men and women, even if he could revise his Epistles in the twentieth century.'[1]

Wives in the same way be submissive to your husbands (v. 1). It is important for us to understand something of the background to Roman family life. Under Roman law the husband and father had absolute authority over every member of his family. If a man became a Christian, then his household would follow him into the church (see Acts 16:29-33). At least in name, they would be a Christian family. In contrast, if a wife believed but her husband did not adopt her faith, then in many respects she would be isolated.

So Peter's exhortation here to believing wives is not unique to the Christian church. The community of the day, both Greek and Roman cultures, required the principle of submission to be followed in the household. It was firmly believed to be for the good of society.

Clowney quotes Plutarch the Greek biographer and moralist, writing in his 'Advice to Bride and Groom' dated not much later than Peter's epistle: 'So it is with women also; if they subordinate themselves to their husbands, they are commended, but if they want to have control, they cut a sorrier figure than the subjects of their control. And control ought to be exercised by the men over the women, not as the owner over a piece of property, but, as the soul controls the body, by entering into her feelings and being knit to her through goodwill.'[2]

It would not commend the Christian church if believers were not prepared to accept patterns which it was felt enhanced the well-being of society, and to follow them might help to silence accusations regarding the lifestyle of believers (2:15). It could possibly even have a more wonderful outcome than that (2:12).

But there are two further and more important reasons why wives should submit; the example of Christ and the Lordship of Christ.

Notice again the phrase which connects with the previous chapter – **in the same way**. Peter has just been writing about the attitude of Christ, and though we make a chapter division, Peter did not. His readers are to mark the spirit of Christ in this. The distinctive behaviour from the wife (and later from the husband, v. 7) is evidence of their relationship to Christ. The world is desperately concerned with its 'rights'; with status and privilege, but these are invariably characteristics of self and selfishness. They are not features which should be evident in the life of the believer. The Christian should not seek after status for its own sake, any more than the humble Christ did (John 13:1-17). He, says Peter, 'entrusted himself to him who judges justly' (2:23). Christ came to serve others and we are to imitate him in all our relationships and not least in the home. What better role model could we have?

But there is also the issue of Christ's Lordship. Notice that even as Jesus knelt before his disciples and washed their feet, he referred to the fact that he was called Lord and 'rightly so for that is what I am' (John 13:13).

The word for **submissive** means 'to place under rank', and the God of order has instituted various levels of authority throughout society. Some of these were referred to in the last chapter (2:13-14). But a person at one level of authority is not necessarily a better person than the one at a lower level. A private in the army is not inferior *as a person* to a colonel; he may in fact be more honourable than the colonel, but in terms of authority he is placed under the colonel. So submission in these verses does not in anyway suggest an inferiority of women and it certainly does not imply that she is to be the man's doormat. How could that be so if these women are **God's elect**? Later Peter refers to *both* husbands and wives, if both are believers, as being **heirs ... of the gracious gift of life (v. 7)**.

The emphasis is always on the different responsibility given to her. She is wife and mother, and God's ordained plan for the home is that the husband should be the team leader. The final responsibility or decision should be his, ideally if a believer, *exercised under the Lordship of Christ.* As Warren Wiersbe says: 'Headship is not dictatorship, but the exercise of divine authority under the Lordship of Christ .... There is nothing degrading in submitting to authority or accepting God's order.'[3]

Therefore a characteristic of the wife should be her subjection to the responsible decisions of her husband. Peter makes it clear that this is not a general instruction for all women to be subject to *all* men. By saying 'to your husbands' he means to their *own* husbands. God has ordained that a man should be the head of his home, and a wife who rebels against that principle, rebels against God.

The distinctiveness of Peter's teaching, as the context makes clear, is the fact that he is writing to some wives who have unbelieving husbands. Paul underlines the same principles of family relationships, but probably has believers in mind (see for example Ephesians 5). Peter is therefore instructing wives who find themselves in this difficult position to follow a similar blueprint, though their husbands may not be believers. He would of course allow the same escape clause which was considered when we looked at their submission to 'every authority instituted among men' (2:13).

Scripture makes it clear that this is the pattern which should be followed, but Peter also indicates a particular and positive outcome which might result for some of his readers – **so that they (husbands) ... may be won over...** This has led to the suggestion that submission was only for this emergency and not required as general practice. However we have already noticed that Paul confirms the same principles in his letters so it is clear that they should apply in all marriages (1 Cor. 11:3-9; Eph. 5:22f.).

Peter expands on the good which can come from the obedience of the wives to God at this point: **so that, if any of them do not believe the word, they may be won over without talk by the behaviour of their wives**. Some husbands, like masters (2:18), may be harsh or as here, those **who do not believe the word**. The verb *apeithein* ('obey not') suggests active hostility to the gospel. One of the problems which a Christian wife would face would be the exclusiveness of her faith. Her unbelieving husband might not object to her believing in the Christian God as well as some of the gods worshipped by the Romans, but he would not understand why she could not and would not serve his gods. He would inevitably see that as a threat to his authority.

Peter encourages wives in this situation that their subjective behaviour will be of more value in winning their husbands than by 'preaching' at them. **Without talk** is a helpful translation because the phrase should not be understood as 'without the word' (that is, the Word of God) since that ultimately is the means of every person's conversion. Christian wives should beware of arguing with, or 'nagging' unsaved husbands, which may serve to drive them further away.

Whilst the principle of submission pertains to all marriages, as we have seen from reference to Paul's epistles, it is clear that the situation envisaged here is where two pagans have married and the wife has afterwards become a believer. Even that marriage, originally between two unbelievers, is not to be broken up when one becomes a believer. Marriage is for life even in those circumstances. Paul says: 'If a woman has a husband who is not a believer and he is willing to live with her, she must not divorce him.... But if the unbeliever leaves, let him do so' (1 Cor. 7:13,15). However neither Peter nor Paul would condone a believer marrying an unbeliever, thus creating this problem. I have performed the marriage ceremony for many believing couples and have been delighted to do so. I have also married a number of couples where neither partner was a believer. I have been prepared to do so because I believe that marriage is an institution ordained by God for the good of society. I have, however, never knowingly married a believer to an unbeliever (2 Cor. 6:14; see also Deut. 22:10).

Many wives today find themselves in the very circumstance which Peter addresses, and even if a mistake has been made with an unequal yoke (2 Cor. 6:14), in addition to repenting of that sin, this advice from Peter is still the best way in which husbands might be won for Christ. Wives should therefore understand that what is commended here is not only the right thing to do, but that their transformed lives can be used to minister to their husbands. Where words from themselves or others may already have failed, in this particular instance 'actions may speak louder than words'. They should not lose hope.

And how does this work out in practice? Peter says it will happen **when they see the purity and reverence of your lives**. These are the attributes which God can use. The word for **see** is linked to the strong word often translated in the Authorised Version by 'behold'. It means 'to watch attentively' or 'to see for yourself'.

Two characteristics in particular will convince them. Purity coupled with reverence. Both are very positive attributes. Purity in her relationship *with* God, out of reverence *for* God.

Your beauty should not come from outward adornment, such as braided hair and the wearing of gold

jewellery and fine clothes (v. 3). Balance is important here. The apostle is not condemning any form of adornment, though in some periods of the church there have been those who have taken his teaching to that extreme. Peter does not condemn adornment outright, since the Creator has made such an attractive world for us to live in and enjoy. The addition of colour for instance, is not essential for us to be able to see, but it has surely been given as a bonus for our pleasure. That seems to confirm the principle that God is not against adornment *per se*. The word for 'adorning' is *kosmos,* which gives us our word 'cosmos', referring to the ordered universe. It also has links with the word 'cosmetic'. God approves of that which is ordered and attractive.

But the extreme is invariably dangerous and was a characteristic of Peter's generation, as it is of our own. For us, addiction to fashion in its various forms – clothes, jewellery, cars and homes is vain. In the area which Peter addresses, a believing wife might feel that she could 'convert' her husband by imitating the fashions of the day. Michael Bentley quotes Kenneth Wuest as saying of Roman wives: 'These women were making the mistake of thinking that if they dressed as the world dressed it would please their unsaved husbands, and the latter would be influenced to trust the Lord Jesus as Saviour. It is true that they would be pleased – pleased because the appearance of their wives appealed to their totally depraved natures and pleased because the Christian testimony of their wives was nullified by their appearance.'[4] Christian wives then and now will not best express their faith by becoming obsessed with fashion; even sometimes adopting what could be the immodest and unrestrained styles of the age. On the other hand a wife should not disregard her appearance. That equally does not speak well of the gospel. It is simply a matter of priorities. Wiersbe confirms that 'Any husband is proud of a wife who is attractive, but that beauty must come from the heart, not from the store.'[5]

The world is primarily concerned with what can be seen

in the outward appearance, and so the thrust of Peter's words is to place emphasis on that which is more valuable i.e. **the inner self**. For example, he seems to suggest that time could be wasted in the braiding of hair etc. to the exclusion of something which is far more profitable.

Instead it should be that of your inner self, the unfading beauty of a gentle and quiet spirit which is of great worth in God's sight (v. 4). Physical beauty though real, is fading, but this beauty continues when the wrinkles begin to show! The word for **unfading** is the same as that used in 1:23 and translated 'imperishable', or incorruptible in reference to the new birth. This inner beauty is evidence of that new life. Here then is the contrast between the outward and the hidden; that which is visible to men and that which is seen by God.

The spiritual qualities referred to are **a gentle and quiet spirit**. The 'spirit' is not the Holy Spirit, but the attributes are certainly the fruit of that Spirit (Gal. 5:22). **Gentle** is the word for meek, i.e. submissive to her husband, not insisting on her rights. It is used in the New Testament as the evidence of a Christlike character (Matt. 5:5). **Quiet** is to be tranquil and calm. This is not only a powerful testimony to the husband but it is also **of great worth in God's sight**. These qualities in the 'inner self' please God.

Peter calls on examples from the past in which these characteristics were true: **For this is the way the holy women of the past who put their hope in God used to make themselves beautiful. They were submissive to their own husbands (v. 5)**. So this advice on how to be truly beautiful does not simply come from a well-meaning male! It has precedents. The example of outstanding wives from the Old Testament can be an inspiration to Christian wives in every generation. They were God's women of that time i.e., **holy ... who put their hope in God**, and part of the outworking of that relationship with God was the conduct they showed toward their husbands. In particular Sarah showed proper deference to her husband (Gen. 18:12), she **obeyed Abraham**

and called him her master (v. 6), even in some situations which might have produced anxiety (Gen. 12:5; 18:6). She recognised his position to have the final word. Clowney points out that 'The Greek term *kyrios* was used in polite address, rather like our "Sir" or "Mr". It indicates the respect with which Sarah spoke of Abraham. Certainly Sarah's submission to Abraham was not slavish.'[6] (See for example Genesis 21:10,12).

You are her daughters if you do what is right and do not give way to fear. Peter tells his readers that their behaviour will show them to be true *spiritual* descendants of Sarah even though some of them were from a pagan and not a Jewish background. But he is not suggesting that theirs is an alternative line to that of Abraham. Abraham and Sarah were those who trusted in God and both are set forth as outstanding examples of faith (Heb. 11:11). God ensured that the promised line should come from Sarah and not from Hagar, so it is not unhelpful to suggest as Stibbs does that 'Just as Abraham is called the father of the faithful, so Sarah may be described as the mother of the obedient'.[7] That surely is what is involved in doing **what is right**.

Peter seems to suggest that sudden fear or panic in the lives of his readers might deny their faith and 'hope in God' (cf. with women of the Old Testament, v. 5). They are Sarah's daughters as they exhibit calm trust in God through any trials and perhaps especially those threats or ill treatment which might be brought on them by unbelieving husbands.

Now Peter turns to the husband and his responsibility: **Husbands, in the same way be considerate as you live with your wives, and treat them with respect as the weaker partner and as heirs with you of the gracious gift of life (v. 7).**

Why did Peter have so much more to say to the wives than to the husbands? Simply because Christian wives in particular had to face very different pressures to their non Christian counterparts. They found themselves on an entirely new footing because of the freedom they now enjoyed in

Christ. In a day when women were generally downtrodden and treated as little more than property, the new standards of the Christian faith placed a strain on marriages and most certainly those in which the husband was an unbeliever. There was also the fact that in this new order a husband now had an obligation to his wife as well as the wife to her husband.

So this message from Peter to husbands is as important as his words to their wives. The **husbands** referred to here are Christian husbands and they are those who **live** or 'dwell' with their wives. Peter seems to be stating the obvious, but he is actually emphasising the physical relationship which should exist between a husband and wife. It has a similar meaning to the word often used in the Old Testament of sexual intercourse, when it was said that a husband 'knew' his wife.

It is interesting that two people sharing the same bed today are said to be 'living together'. Peter has a similar idea in mind, but of course in the context of marriage. Paul confirms that in marriage 'the two will become one flesh' (Eph. 5:31). Mutual love is expressed as they fulfil their marital duties to each other (1 Cor. 7:1-7).

But surely part of the practical outworking of that will be broader than the sexual relationship. It will find husbands making time for their families rather than being at work most hours of the day – and then at church most hours of the night! And ideally it will also include the principle that it is the husband's responsibility to provide for the practical needs of the family. All of this and more is true for those who are 'living *together*'.

There is to be consideration of the wife as the weaker partner. The husband is to do his best to know and to understand his wife, recognising her special needs. That is the meaning of the word **considerate** or 'according to knowledge' (AV). The reason for this is that she usually has the more delicate physical frame, though mentally and morally and even spiritually she may be stronger. She will look for protection from her husband and only in this mutual trust will the marriage be successful.

The husband will not belittle his wife. He will **treat (her) with respect**. The idea of 'honour' (AV) is helpful since it has a stronger tone than 'respect'. The wife is a partner and has a point of view which should be heard. Husbands are not infallible. Indeed their combined effort might produce the best solution. Warren Wiersbe suggests that 'the husband must be the "thermostat" in the home, setting the emotional and spiritual temperature. The wife often is the "thermometer", letting him know what the temperature is!'[8]

Before God they are absolute equals. Husbands are reminded that their wives are **heirs with you of the gracious gift of life**. They have been called together into this joint partnership of fellowship with God. They enjoy the marvellous privileges and prospects which make up eternal life. The principles set out by Peter are relevant in any generation, but in the culture of that day where marriage was not considered the *partnership* that it is today, at least in our Western society, we can see how particularly applicable it was to his readers.

One test as to whether a Christian marriage is successful is the fact that husband and wife pray together. Something is wrong in a Christian marriage if they do not share prayer together. Peter assumes that they will, but indicates that if all is not well in the relationship, then their prayer life will be affected. They will literally find the way blocked; the relationship must therefore be on the right footing **so that nothing will hinder your prayers**. The Greek verb *enkoptein* is the word that would be used for making a road impassable.

Stibbs confirms the fact that 'Human disharmony can upset spiritual cooperation'.[9] The Life Application Bible comments that 'a living relationship with God depends on a right relationship with others'. We could add that the reverse is equally true – a right relationship with others depends on a living relationship with God. How many marriages might have been preserved and would certainly have been improved, if husbands and wives had prayed together from the beginning.

So then this is the pattern for a successful marriage. The wife is to be submissive to her husband and the husband is to respect or honour his wife. Paul puts it in a slightly different way when he uses the picture of marriage to illustrate the mysterious relationship which exists between Christ and the church, and then says, 'each one of you also must love his wife as he loves himself, and the wife must respect her husband' (Eph. 5:32,33).

Neither will take advantage of each other or manipulate each other, and together with God they become the ideal team which he has brought together.

2. SYMPATHY (verses 8-17)

Finally, all of you, live in harmony with one another; be sympathetic, love as brothers, be compassionate and humble (v. 8). Finally does not suggest the end of the epistle, merely the conclusion of this particular section. Peter has dealt with a variety of relationships, now follows this general exhortation to all and it should not surprise us that the underlying theme is love. There are five characteristics in particular.

They should **live in harmony with one another**. This means literally 'being of one mind'. But harmony does not mean that everyone is singing exactly the same tune! We are different, but we should all have the mind of Christ, so any differences which we express because of what we are and where we have come from should add richness to the church not division. Wiersbe says: 'Unity does not mean uniformity; it means cooperation in the midst of diversity. The members of the body work together in unity, even though they are different. Christians may differ on *how* things are to be done, but they must agree on *what* is to be done and *why*.'[10] If yours is a church that has a members' roll and convenes business meetings, you will know that there are always more potential dangers at that meeting than at any other event in the calendar of the church!

Christians should be like-minded because they have a common source to instruct the mind and that is the Word of God. The emphasis is on an agreement reached by all receiving the truth of God through his Word. The priority therefore is to know the mind of Christ, rather than take a straw poll from a diversity of human minds.

Peter himself had been told by the Lord that he did 'not have in mind the things of God, but the things of men' (Matt. 16:23). He had taken the Lord aside and told him that he was not to do his Father's will, that he Peter, would not allow him to suffer and die. The word for 'mind' in the Lord's reply is the same as **harmony** here. I have no doubt Peter had this in his thoughts as he wrote these words.

It was certainly important for these first century believers to know that their aims and purposes were in harmony as they faced persecution together.

Then they must **be sympathetic**. They should enter into another's feelings as if they were their own. These may be both joys and sorrows. For believers to have an interest in others will be in direct contrast to unbelievers who are more often than not, characterised by selfishness.

They must **love as brothers**. The English language has a saying that 'blood is thicker than water', suggesting the special tie which holds a family together. Believers have a similar link, but through blood which is far more precious. By grace we are brothers and sisters in the family of God (1:17, 22). There may be occasions when we do not agree and even aggravate each other as can happen in any family. Yet the 'tie that binds our hearts in Christian love' should still be in evidence.

They must **be compassionate**. What a powerful emotion this can be. The root of the word has connections with the inner organs of the body. So it speaks of our innermost feelings. It means 'pity' in its very best sense which was not considered a positive attribute in the Roman world. Therefore this was something else which set the Christian religion apart.

Today much is made of the merit of allowing our feelings

to be expressed. Following the death of the Princess of Wales, senior royals in Britain were heavily criticised by many because they preferred to grieve in private, in contrast to the very public outpouring of grief shown by the masses. Some journalists have referred disparagingly to an 'emotional incontinence' which in the last year or so has swept the western world, more used to the 'stiff upper lip'. While some of us too may draw back from this kind of 'emotionalism' it must not deter us from feeling and expressing genuine compassion for those who suffer. In this again our Lord has set us a wonderful example (Matt. 9:36; Mark 8:2; James 5:11).

They should be **humble**. This means 'lowly minded' which would reflect itself in mutual subjection to each other. If the Romans rejected the idea of pity, then the Greeks could not understand humility. To them it was a sign of weakness. One characteristic which has to be present in every believer is the recognition that whatever good we have, we have received by the grace of God. We have no reason to set ourselves above a fellow believer. Our abysmal failure in the past and the frailty of our natural abilities in the present leave us no room for pride. However we must be careful to avoid a false humility which is almost as objectionable. It is strange but true that it is possible to be humble and proud of it! I like the way Stuart Briscoe expresses the truth behind this word: 'To be humble-minded is to have a realistic appraisal of ourselves before God.'[11] Michael Bentley quotes Chuck Swindoll from one of his radio programmes: 'You can fake love, you can fake patience, you can fake tolerance, you can fake wealth or poverty but you cannot fake humility.... Humility is the fairest flower that blooms; but display it once and it withers into pride.... There is no way you can write a book called, *How I achieved humility,* or a sequel entitled, *How I regained humility.*'[12]

Peter later (5:5) underlines the importance of humility by quoting from Proverbs 3:34. It was another lesson he had learned the hard way.

Like-mindedness, sympathy, brotherly love, compassion and humility. How beautifully these five characteristics reflect the life and teaching of the Lord we profess to follow.

These instructions are particularly for relationships with those within the family of God. Now Peter makes reference to our attitude to those outside of the faith, though I venture to suggest that this response is sometimes necessary *within* the church!

Do not repay evil with evil or insult with insult, but with blessing (v. 9). Peter tells us here how Christians 'get even'! Speaking well of those who speak ill of us is demanding. There are easier options. Warren Wiersbe helpfully suggests that as Christians we can live on three levels: 'We can return evil for good, which is the Satanic level. We can return good for good and evil for evil, which is the human level. Or, we can return good for evil, which is the divine level. Jesus is the perfect example of this latter approach (2:21-23).'[13] Peter has already written: 'When they hurled their insults at him, he did not retaliate; when he suffered, he made no threats. Instead, he entrusted himself to him who judges justly' (2:23).

The word for **blessing** (*eulogountes*) means to seek a person's highest good. The connection with eulogy is obvious but eulogising should not wait until a person is gone. Whatever people say of us we must bless them because we wish the very best for them; that is, we wish God's best for them! We may have no direct means by which we can bestow a blessing on them, but we can pray that God will do for them that which is outside of our power. Clowney reminds us of the occasion when Stephen prayed for those who stoned him: 'Lord, do not hold this sin against them' (Acts 7:60). A young Pharisee named Saul was one of those for whom Stephen prayed and the Lord answered that prayer![14]

Some feel that the word may include a positive conferring of benefits. Our response might therefore sometimes include a tangible gift!

The Christian should always be more concerned with mercy for others than he is with justice for himself. Stibbs writes: 'In Christ God blesses those who have sinned against Him. It is therefore an essential part of our Christian calling ourselves to experience the kind of treatment which we are here exhorted to give to those who sin against us.'[15]

Peter reminds them that this is behind the calling of every believer – **because to this you were called so that you might inherit a blessing**. They understood that in becoming Christians they would have to act in this way, and the fact that they were **called** confirms that the inheritance is secure (1:4). The use of the word **inherit** indicates that this is a gift, and not a blessing they have earned or deserved.

They might also remember that not every blessing which they are to inherit is in the future. A blessing bestowed on someone else, brings an immediate blessing to them. The experience of every believer in every generation who has practised this precept confirms the truth of it.

So even in their severe trials there are still greater spiritual blessings to be received and sometimes in unexpected ways. They and we should remember that the world's view of 'good times' will be different to the view which God has. Many of Peter's readers will suffer greatly. The Acts of the Apostles provides some background to the pain which first century Christians had to face, but who would doubt that Paul and Silas, for example, would look back on those days as anything other than 'good times.' Peter now provides more information on how to enjoy **good days**.

He quotes from Psalm 34:12-16 to illustrate and underline these important lessons: **For, 'Whoever would love life and see good days must keep his tongue from evil and his lips from deceitful speech' (v. 10)**. Bible scholars suggest that sections of this Psalm were probably used as a catechism or hymn in regular worship. Peter adapts the Psalm to bring out additional truth. The Psalm speaks of a man who wants a long and happy life, whereas Peter's emphasis is more on the

man who wants to **love life and see good days**. That person
must, the emphasis is on the will, refrain from every evil of
the tongue whether it be slander, obscenity or lies. So much
evil is expressed, and so much pain is caused by the misuse
of the tongue. Peter more than most, had learned this lesson
but we could all benefit by following the advice of James on
the training of the tongue (ch. 3).

Nor should there be anything in our speech which is
deliberately calculated to mislead. Peter speaks of **deceitful
speech**. Lies, even so-called 'white lies' are anathema for
the Christian, not least because they never passed the lips of
our Master, for 'no deceit was found in his mouth' (2:22).

Then, not only are a believer's words to be above reproach,
his deeds too, must be blameless: **He must turn from evil
and do good; he must seek peace and pursue it (v. 11)**. He
must avoid or 'eschew' (AV) evil, that is he must 'swerve out
of the way' of it, and positively endeavour to do good. Notice
again the emphasis on disciplining the will in these areas.

The 'peace' we desire must be the subject of a careful
search. If someone is 'looking for trouble' he will probably
find it. Equally it is possible to search for peace and find it,
because the Christian should not be constantly wanting to
get his own way, on the motorway, in the supermarket, in
business or in the family. Paul underlined this important
principle. 'If it is possible, as far as it depends on you, live at
peace with everyone' (Rom. 12:18). The Lord himself had
previously included this as part of his pattern for blessing
(Matt. 5:9), and it is in any case an outworking of our
salvation, which was procured firstly to reconcile man with
God and then to harmonise man with his fellow. In this way
the two greatest commandments are obeyed; to love both God
and man (Matt. 22:37-39).

To follow the principles which the Psalmist provides and
which Peter confirms, may even help you to live longer by
reducing your blood pressure! There may be nothing wrong
in 'living it up' as long as that means avoiding evil in word

or deed and pursuing peace. There is no better way to live life to its fullest than to live it for God in this way.

Remember the situation into which Peter sends this message. This is the way he says, to **love life and see good days**, notwithstanding your circumstances, because the Lord has those in mind.

For the eyes of the Lord are on the righteous and his ears are attentive to their prayer (v. 12). The fact that the Lord's eyes are on us should be sufficient reason for self restraint under provocation. Equally to know that the One who suffered in a similar yet greater way, is watching, not only makes self defence unnecessary but we should be ashamed to use it.

Peter's major emphasis is the fact that the eyes of the Lord are on the righteous *for good* and that **his ears are attentive to their prayer**. Attributing physical features to a God who is Spirit simply serves to illustrate the intimacy of their relationship with him. Such is the availability of this God that we can go to him at any time.

But the face of the Lord is against those who do evil. When we enter into prayer we sometimes refer to 'seeking God's face'. This is biblical language which implies God turning his face *toward* us. Alternatively when God is displeased he turns his face *away*. Here there is divine disapproval of those who do evil. The original in the Psalm, which Peter excludes, adds a determination to punish (Ps. 34:16).

Who is going to harm you if you are eager to do good? (v. 13). Ellicott, using the Authorised Version writes: 'There is always a ring of scornful assurance in an interrogative introduced by "And, who pray".'[16]

In general terms this principle which Peter presents is true, but this does seem a strange thing to write to people who at that time were already suffering for doing good! Their experiences told them that there are many who are prepared to harm those who are doing good!

The truth is this. Though men and devils may do their

best to hurt them, as they did Christ, they cannot harm them in the sense that no evil can touch them. The New International Version misses this by omitting the 'And' at the beginning of the sentence which would give the sense of 'then', and thus link with the assurance in the previous verse which promises them that the Lord watches over them and cares for them. Our thoughts go immediately to Paul's great affirmation concerning a Christian's security: 'If God is for us, who can be against us?' (Rom. 8:31). Or again, to the response of the believer to the statement from God, ' "Never will I leave you; never will I forsake you." ... we say with confidence, "The Lord is my helper; I will not be afraid. What can man do to me?" ' (Heb. 13:5-6). Nothing can separate the believer from the love of Christ and his place in heaven is assured, therefore nothing which is temporal can prejudice that which is eternal (Rom. 8:38-39).

But surely implicit in Peter's words is some good practical advice. Although foremost in his mind is the suffering that comes to believers because of their faith, could he not also be making the general point that those who live a life of benevolence and integrity can enjoy a measure of escape from many of the pressures which would affect the opposite type of personality? Driving consistently within the law will reduce the possibility of an accident. Cultivating a good relationship with my wife and children will help to create a happy and peaceful home.

But even if you should suffer for what is right, you are blessed. 'Do not fear what they fear; do not be frightened' (v. 14). Peter later underscores the fact that believers should not think it strange that they suffer persecution (4:12). It is not only possible, but it is probable that Christians are going to suffer. Jesus said it, and the apostles underlined it (John 16:33). When this happens, says Peter, it is not only to be regarded as a privilege but also as a means of positive blessing to them. He uses the same word (*makarioi*) which Jesus used in the Beatitudes. In the Scripture, **blessed** always indicates a divine favour bestowed on us. Clowney makes the very helpful point that Christians 'must understand that suffering is not the opposite of blessing. Jesus had declared those to be blessed who suffer for righteousness (Matt. 5:10-12).'[17]

This is in direct contrast to the world's attitude to suffering, which believes it is being unfairly treated. Indeed not all pain is bad. Sometimes it is good because it serves as a warning, particularly in the body. We should therefore beware of the world's judgment which pronounces that all that is 'pleasurable' is good and all that is 'painful' is bad.

Do not fear what they fear is a quotation from Isaiah 8:12. The exhortation from Isaiah is to Ahaz King of Judah not to form an unholy alliance with Assyria because of pressure imposed upon him by Israel and Syria. It could have a similar meaning here since there may have been pressure on some Christians to join in emperor worship or revert to heathen idolatry. Notice how Isaiah continued, 'The LORD Almighty is the one you are to regard as holy, he is the one you are to fear, he is the one you are to dread' (Isa. 8:13). Peter takes a similar line in using the word **fear** in both a negative and positive way. They are not to be afraid of what others might do but they are to show reverence and respect for God. Bentley says: 'The negative meaning is the one which we normally associate with the word "fear." The positive aspect is the same as what we declare when we say in the Lord's Prayer, "Hallowed be your name" (Matthew 6:9).'[18]

Peter underlines this truth by linking his reference to the Lord Almighty, with Jesus Christ: **But in your hearts set apart Christ Jesus as Lord (v. 15)**. This sentence gives the sense as follows: 'In your hearts, or in the affections of your soul, set apart the Lord Christ as the Holy One'. If we acknowledge Christ as Lord and act in that way toward him then we have no need to fear men. The Christian should be more fearful of displeasing the Lord, than he is afraid of those who might hurt him. The hymn writer expresses it in this quaint but helpful way:

Fear Him, ye saints, and you will then
Have nothing else to fear;
Make you His service your delight,
Your wants shall be His care.

This in turn can provide opportunities for the spread of
the gospel. A Christian's response to suffering, so different
to the world's, will eventually draw questions. Their attitude
when under pressure will make others take notice, so **Always
be prepared to give an answer to everyone who asks you
to give the reason for the hope you have. But do this with
gentleness and respect**.

The Christian might be asked at any time to explain his
'hope' and not least in hopeless situations. As Clowney says,
'Peter sees the "impossible" position of Christians as a
remarkable opportunity to bear witness to Christ.'[19] Not every
Christian is a theologian or apologist for every aspect of truth,
but he (or she) should have an intelligent grasp of his 'hope'
in order to answer the questions which may be asked, and the
emphasis here is on his readiness to do so. We are **always** to
be prepared to give an answer to **everyone**. This is to be done
courteously, without arrogance or self assertion. What might
have been a wonderful opportunity for witness has so often
been spoilt by a Christian's conceit or smugness. Wiersbe
comments: 'We are witnesses, not prosecuting attorneys!'[20]
We are primarily concerned with winning a soul not winning
an argument. Paul expresses a similar truth: 'Be wise in the
way you act towards outsiders; make the most of every
opportunity. Let your conversation be always full of grace,
seasoned with salt, so that you may know how to answer
everyone' (Col. 4:5-6).

The Greek word for 'respect' is *phobos* which means 'fear',
suggesting that whereas the **gentleness** is in regard to men,
respect or 'fear' refers to reverence of God. Peter thinks again
of Isaiah 8:13 – 'he is the one you are to fear.'

Part of our God-given make-up is the fact that human

beings are born with a conscience; an ability to discern right
from wrong. Even though that conscience has been corrupted
by sin and is therefore unreliable, how disturbing that
conscience can be, and what a good thing that it is. Peter
speaks here of **keeping a clear conscience, so that those
who speak maliciously against your good behaviour in
Christ may be ashamed of their slander**. The conscience
is safe to be trusted only when the mind has been renewed,
but that is exactly the condition the believer is in. He can
discern the will of God from his study of the Scriptures which
will make him sensitive to what is right and wrong in God's
eyes. This clearly indicates the value and importance of the
believer spending time with the Scriptures in order that his
mind and heart might be instructed in those things which
please God so that he will not knowingly say or do anything
which would affect his testimony.

Peter is referring here to those who speak against **good**
behaviour. We should be aware of the importance of the
believer's *life* always confirming what his *lips* profess. There
must never be a credibility gap, i.e., a difference between
what we say and what we do. If the world speaks maliciously
against good behaviour, they will certainly see through
hypocrisy and despise it.

Yet even when our actions are blameless, inevitably there
will be those who will speak evil of us. Wiersbe makes the
point that though 'as a rule Christians do not *create* problems;
they *reveal* them.'[21] A Christian working in an office and
endeavouring to live according to God's standards, will
eventually antagonise some of those around him. One
commentator makes the valid point that the world dislikes
those that are too bad and equally those that are too good.
Notice how many of God's servants in Scripture had conflict
in their lives because they 'revealed' the corruptness of their
society, often simply by the way they lived. It was supremely
true in the life of the Lord Jesus Christ.

Our conduct in Christ will eventually put them to silence

if not now, certainly on the Day of Judgment. Peter began this thought in 2:11 and continues it here. Plato the Greek philosopher was told that someone was making slanderous accusations against him. His response was, 'I will live in such a way that no one will believe what he says.'[22]

It is better, if it is God's will, to suffer for doing good than for doing evil (v. 17). If we suffer for doing wrong we are only experiencing the consequences which our actions deserve, but if a *good* God allows doers of *good* to suffer it must be for a *good* reason. And the truth is even more powerful than that. If God is Sovereign and he is, then he not only permits suffering he ordains it by initiating testing and trial for his own good purposes and our ultimate blessing! Sometimes neither we nor others will be able to see the logic or sense of it at the time. The experience of Job amongst others, confirms this. Throughout Scripture we are shown that we are dealing with a unique God. 'For my thoughts are not your thoughts, neither are your ways my ways, declares the Lord. As the heavens are higher than the earth, so are my ways higher than your ways and my thoughts than your thoughts' (Isa. 55:8,9).

Peter says that it is God's will that believers should suffer for doing good! This adds a whole new dimension to the subject of suffering. Peter makes it a plus point. If we are to suffer, he says, let it be by the direct hand of God and not through any fault of our own.

The perfect example of this is of course the Lord himself, and Peter now turns to look at his suffering in more detail. This verse therefore stands as a foundation for the verses that follow. Remember that the overall message which Peter is presenting is the fact that *blessing* follows suffering for doing good.

3. SUFFERING (verses 18-22)

Peter has already outlined two necessities of suffering in the Christian's experience. It should be undeserved and it should be divinely ordained. This is supremely illustrated in the suffering of Christ: **For Christ died for sins once for all, the righteous for the unrighteous, to bring you to God (v. 18).** Here is as clear an explanation as we can find in the New Testament, and from someone who knew him well, as to the meaning of the death of Christ. The word 'suffered' as used in the Authorised Version literally means 'died'.

Human assessment of Christ's death might suggest that the One who was so good, died unjustly. The truth is that he was not dying for himself but for others. He was dying for those who were *not* good. He was dying for sinners. Therefore the fact that he was innocent and yet suffered, makes him a good example for all who suffer for well doing.

Peter makes a number of important points in this statement. First as we have already underlined, the death of Christ was **for sins,** that is *for sinners.* Sin is serious, separating us from God in time and eternity (Isa. 59:2). Man has no means of his own to provide forgiveness. If someone steals from me, I can offer to forgive him, but he cannot respond by suggesting that I do not need to offer forgiveness, because he has already forgiven himself! That is a nonsense. Nor can any third party who is not involved, forgive him. That is equally ridiculous. Yet there are some people who depend either on their ability to console their own conscience or alternatively to trust in a forgiveness which is pronounced on them by a third party. But God is the One offended! It is *his* law which has been broken. Any possible forgiveness can only come from his direction. When the teachers of the law criticised Jesus because he forgave a man his sins, their statement was perfectly correct: 'Who can forgive sins, except God alone?' Their problem was that they did not believe that Jesus was God and therefore able to do that, nor even allowed to suggest that he could (Mark 2:7). God is able and willing to forgive sin, says Peter. That is why Christ died.

The second point that Peter makes is that the death of Jesus was *as a substitute* – **the righteous for the unrighteous**. Christ had lived the perfect life. In every respect he was righteous, that is perfectly acceptable before God. This was the relevance, value and importance of the life he lived out here on earth. He was, as Martin Luther said, 'The Proper Man'. But he died for those who were not right with God in taking their place and bearing their punishment. He provided the ground on which God can justly forgive sin.

Peter also confirms that this his death was *sufficient*. What Christ did, he did **once for all**. Many sacrifices had been offered throughout the Old Testament age, being types or patterns of Christ's sacrifice. Now no further sacrifice is needed because his was a sufficient, complete and finished work, confirmed by his resurrection from the dead. His death fully meets the demands that the justice of God required for sin. Mrs Alexander expressed this in a beautiful way.

> He died that we might be forgiven,
> He died to make us good,
> That we might go at last to heaven,
> Saved by His precious blood.
>
> There was no other good enough
> To pay the price of sin;
> He only could unlock the gate
> Of heaven, and let us in.

The ultimate purpose was **to bring you to God**, that is, to reconcile sinful men with a holy God. To bring back together two parties who had been separated. God had created man for a special purpose which could not be fulfilled by any other part of creation. Man was made in the image of God (Gen. 1:26-27), which means that he was able to relate to God in love, obedience, worship and service. That special relationship was enjoyed by our first parents for a time, but when sin was introduced at the Fall, God became inaccessible to man except on new terms which God set down. These were symbolised in the Temple where a huge and heavy curtain separated the people from God's presence (Exod. 26:33-34). The High Priest alone was able to enter this holiest place of all, and only at certain times. The curtain remained in place through generations until it was torn from top to bottom at the time of Christ's death (Luke 23:45). The means of reconciliation had been provided. The curtain could be removed. A new way into the presence of God was available through Christ. Justice had been satisfied. The merit which accrues from Christ's death requires no compromise from God.

Reconciliation in most walks of life usually requires concession from both parties. That is certainly true in the political, industrial and domestic arenas. But the death of Christ does not bring God to us in a spirit of compromise, it brings us to God in a spirit of confession. God is not required to 'give a little' because he has already given much. 'For God so loved the world that he gave his one and only Son, that whoever believes in him shall not perish but have eternal life. For God did not send his Son into the world to condemn the world, but to save the world through him' (John 3:16,17). Ellicott writes: 'There is no appeal which can be made to us more powerful than the one drawn from the fact that another suffers on our account. We could resist the argument which a father or mother or sister would use to reclaim us from a course of sin. But if we perceive that our conduct involves them in suffering that fact has a power over us which no mere argument could have.'[23]

He was put to death in the body but made alive by the Spirit. To **put to death** suggests a brutal end. Man has rarely contrived a more cruel means of execution than by Roman crucifixion.

So Christ was put to death as far as his body was concerned, that is, he died, but he was **made alive by the Spirit**. Because in Greek there were no capitals in the manuscripts some would say that there is no authority for adding the capital letter to the word 'spirit'. Therefore some scholars suggest that this is not a direct reference to the Holy Spirit. Peter, we are told, could be referring to Christ's human spirit and if he is, then he is indicating that following his death Christ's spirit was reanimated to life on a new level. This argument is strengthened when it is understood that the prepositions 'in' and 'by' were not present in the original. Therefore 'in' could be used in both phrases. Though his body therefore remained in the tomb, later to be resurrected and reunited with his spirit, the spirit was free for a period. And as a spirit set free he was able to operate in the spiritual realm. If this is accepted as the correct interpretation then it will have a bearing on our understanding of the next few verses.

Through whom also he went and preached to the spirits in prison who disobeyed long ago when God waited patiently in the days of Noah while the ark was being built (vv. 19-20). These verses are some of the most difficult in the New Testament to interpret accurately. A number of commentators refer to Martin Luther's words: 'A wonderful text is this, and a more obscure passage perhaps than any other in the New Testament, so that I do not know for a certainty just what Peter means.' That should prompt us to be cautious!

We do need to tread carefully since the Roman doctrine of purgatory finds some basis in these verses, and we can see how easy it would be to fall into that trap.

One suggested interpretation is that Christ actually went to the spirits of lost sinners in hell, there to preach the gospel to them. This I believe to be the weakest explanation, not least because it suggests the possibility that purgatory does exist. To avoid this some scholars tell us that the word 'preach' here does not have a direct link with the truth or the gospel, rather Peter uses the other more neutral word also translated 'preach' which means to proclaim, or make an announcement like a herald or town crier.

But why should these unbelievers *in particular* have this

privilege? What of others prior to them, and millions since, who do not appear to have had that opportunity?

And how does their experience relate directly to Peter's purpose here, which is to show his readers that suffering for a good cause, and with the right spirit works for their blessing?

Peter tells us that Jesus went where evil spirits were in prison; they were in captivity. But this is not hell, the final destination after judgment, rather Hades the temporary place prior to judgment. Wiersbe points out that a careful reading of Revelation 20:11-15 provides a helpful and important distinction for our understanding of these two words.[24] Those who accept the interpretation as stated above, believe that Peter indicates that these spirits were involved in some way in the great wickedness which occurred before the flood. They say it may or may not be those referred to in Genesis 6:1-4.

Many Bible scholars admit to great difficulties in accepting this interpretation.

An alternative explanation is set out by Alan Stibbs. He suggests that the freedom which the spirit of Christ had, enabled him to 'go where evil spirits are in prison awaiting the judgment of the great day' (2 Peter 2:4,5; Jude 6), and to announce to them His victory over death, and over the consequences to men of their evil doing. He thus made them aware that their own judgment was finally sealed.'[25] Here the emphasis is not on the preaching of the gospel with an opportunity to respond but rather a statement of condemnation, in view of his victory over sin.

Augustine held to an entirely different interpretation since he believed that Christ's preaching was done *through* Noah in his time, *by* Christ's Spirit. Those people were not literally in prison of course though spiritually they could have been described in that way.

Another quite different suggestion comes from John Brown who believes this is a reference to what Christ did on the Day of Pentecost when by his Spirit and in his complete victory, he spoke spiritually to captives in prison i.e. men bound by sin. He feels that the reference to Noah is not an insurmountable problem since they are given as illustrations of men's disobedience through the ages, and because Peter wants to use that particular age to illustrate a further point.[26]

There is one further theory which I believe has merit. It is a slight variation of Augustine's position and helps to remove a little of the mystery in Peter's words. It is borne out by a straightforward reading of the New International Version text which refers to something that Christ did by his Spirit (notice the **through whom**), but through Noah as a 'preacher of righteousness' (2 Peter 2:5), to those who were disobedient in Noah's day and are *now* 'spirits in prison', that is because of their disobedience at *that* time.

The reference then in verse 18 to Christ being **made alive by the Spirit** would refer not to a disembodied Christ but to his risen life (Rom. 8:11).

Whichever interpretation we prefer does not in any way undermine the main lessons of the passage. Brown makes this observation: 'though we should not be able to determine with absolute certainty who these spirits in prison are, and when, and where, and how, and for what purpose, Christ went and preached to them; and whatever opinion we may adopt as most probable on these subjects, no Christian doctrine, no Christian duty, is affected by our uncertainty or by our opinion.'[27] Not even the Roman doctrine of purgatory nor any belief in universalism can be built on these verses, since Scripture as a whole does not support those ideas.

Peter uses the connection with Noah and the ark to make another important point. **In it only a few people, eight in all, were saved through water**. He is going to link the ark with the present day and show how the blessing enjoyed by Noah's relatives, few though they were, is similar to the blessings enjoyed by his readers, however few they may be.

The ark has always been a wonderful picture of salvation. The eight who were saved were brought safely through by water. Peter does not say that they were saved *from* water but *through* it since the same water that drowned the disobedient brought the others to safety because it floated their ark and brought them into a new experience.

Now **water** provides the link into baptism: **and this water symbolises baptism that now saves you also – not the removal of dirt from the body but the pledge of a good conscience toward God (v. 21)**. Just as water saved Noah and his family by bearing them above the flood, so water in the form of baptism saves us now. Peter is very quick to make the point that it is not the water itself, but that which baptism symbolises i.e. repentance toward God and faith in our Lord Jesus Christ. Baptism is a serious step which indicates a great truth. It is a picture of death, burial and resurrection to new life and so not only reflects what physically happened to Christ but also the work of the Spirit in every believer's life. It is much more than a ceremony which provides admission to the church.

The **pledge** is thought to be the examination which was necessary prior to baptism. It was a pronouncement of a candidate's resolve to put off the old life and to begin a new life in Christ and was usually conducted in a question and answer form. Those answers would articulate very clearly exactly what they were professing. Peter reminds them of this since that faith will be put to the test by persecution.

Peter states the truth which is the foundation of their faith, and not the rite of baptism itself: **It saves you by the resurrection of Jesus Christ**. If Christ had not been raised from the dead, baptism would have no value, in fact it would make no sense. The resurrection of Christ confirms his credentials and proves that his accusers were wrong to suggest that he was an imposter and blasphemer. Says Paul, he 'was declared with power to be the Son of God by his resurrection from the dead' (Rom. 1:4). The resurrection also speaks of his complete victory over sin and death.

And this was followed by his triumphant return to heaven. Peter says that Christ has gone into heaven and is at God's right hand – with angels, authorities and powers in submission to him (v. 22). It is the Man Jesus Christ who has gone **into heaven** and who **is at God's right hand**. Notice the present tense. He is the One who is now entirely victorious, with everything and everyone subject to his control.

Clowney makes the following comment on this passage: 'Persecuted and suffering Christians need to remember both the humiliation and the exaltation of Christ. His patient suffering will show them meekness when they are interrogated. His glorious triumph will give them courage to face their accusers. Undergirding both the meekness and the boldness of the Christian is the saving work of Christ.'[28]

Chuck Swindoll suggests two practical principles we can draw from this part of Peter's epistle. First, when unjust suffering seems unbearable, remember the crucifixion. Second, when the fear of death steals your peace, remember the resurrection.[29] This is what gives the Christian hope even when in the middle of trials!

References

1. Wayne Detzler, *Living Words in 1 Peter*, Evangelical Press, 1982, p. 60.
2. Edmund P. Clowney, *The Message of 1 Peter*, IVP, 1988, p. 127.
3. Warren Wiersbe, *Be Hopeful*, Victor Books, 1982, pp. 75,76.
4. Michael Bentley, *Living for Christ in a Pagan World*, Evangelical Press, 1990, p. 112.
5. Wiersbe, p. 79.
6. Clowney, p. 133.
7. A. M. Stibbs, *I Peter*, Tyndale Commentaries, 1959, p. 126.
8. Wiersbe, p. 82.
9. Stibbs, p. 127.
10. Wiersbe, p. 86.
11. Stuart Briscoe, *Holy Living in a Hostile World*, Harold Shaw, 1982, p. 133.
12. Bentley, p. 126.
13. Wiersbe, p. 87.

14. Clowney, p. 141.

15. Stibbs, p. 131.

16. Charles Ellicott, *New Testament Commentary*, 1897, p. 417.

17. Clowney, p. 144.

18. Bentley, p. 130.

19. Clowney, p. 129.

20. Wiersbe, p. 91

21. Wiersbe, p. 94

22. William Barclay, The Daily Study Bible Series, Westminster Press, 1975, p 203.

23. Ellicott, ibid.

24. Wiersbe, p. 99.

25. Stibbs, p. 142.

26. John Brown, *I Peter*, Banner of Truth, 1975, p. 204.

27. Brown, p. 192.

28. Clowney, p. 155.

29. Chuck Swindoll, *Hope Again*, Word, 1996, p. 159.

CHAPTER
FOUR

THE REST OF
OUR LIVES

Having set out the principles behind the cross of Christ, Peter looks now at its practical application. How should this apply in the lives of his readers? The word 'therefore' in the Scriptures invariably provides the method of linking principles with practice.

Peter now understood the relevance of the cross of Christ. That had not always been the case. During those early days of discipleship none of our Lord's followers had grasped the significance of who he was and particularly what he was to do, least of all Peter. On one occasion which he would now prefer to forget, he had even forbidden the Lord to go up to Jerusalem and to death, and had been rebuked in the strongest possible terms (Matt. 16:21-22). Peter, with his traditional thoughts of a Jewish Messiah, had been making plans for a kingdom not a cross. Then again, with the sincerest of motives and to defend his Lord, he had physically stepped between Christ and the cross by cutting off the ear of Malchus, the servant of the high priest who had been sent to arrest Jesus. Peter is chastened as he gets it wrong again (Luke 22:50-51). All of this is compounded by his denial and subsequent despair. After the resurrection Jesus meets privately with Peter and gently questions his love (John 21:15-19). Gradually the truth begins to dawn and when the apostles preach the gospel on the Day of Pentecost, Peter is their spokesman. He declares with heart and voice: 'This man (Jesus) was handed over to you by God's set purpose and foreknowledge; and you, with the help of wicked men, put him to death by nailing him to a cross. But God raised him from the dead...' (Acts 2:23-24).

Peter can apply the message of the cross, because now he understands it. If a person does not understand the cross of Christ he will not appreciate the demands which that cross makes on him. Stuart Briscoe draws attention to those today who want a Christ of their own making, in just the way Peter did. 'But a Christ who has a cross is totally repugnant to them. Like Peter, they won't even let Christ have a cross – let alone take up one themselves.'[1]

117

1. SANCTIFICATION (verses 1-6)

Having written about the suffering of his Lord, Peter now presents this challenge to his readers: **Therefore since Christ suffered in his body, arm yourselves also with the same attitude (v. 1).** This is a link back to 3:18. **Since Christ suffered** (and we have already noticed that the word in relation to Christ means 'died'), **arm yourselves also...** The use of the military metaphor underlines the fact that we are in a battle. If we don't recognise that from the start, then we are heading for defeat in our Christian lives!

Peter speaks here of an attitude of mind with which Christ armed himself. But in relation to what?

Peter has presented clear teaching on the fact of, need for and purpose of the death of Christ. 'Christ died *for sins*', he tells us (3:18) and is now 'done with sin'. This does not mean that Jesus then stopped sinning, since at no time had he ever been a sinner (2:22). What Peter does mean is that at the cross Christ assumed our sin, dealt with it, and is now finished with sin forever. His work was 'once for all', Peter has told us (3:18). Clowney points out that the formation of the Greek for 'done with sin' – 'describes a present condition determined by a past event.'[2]

Now we are to adopt a similar attitude: **he who has suffered in his body is done with sin**. Again Peter is not suggesting here that earthly suffering will stop anyone sinning. Suffering of itself will not produce sinlessness, in fact in the case of some without Christ it may even increase guilt, as they curse God because of their circumstances.

Perhaps we can best understand it in this way. A physically dead person is delivered from any further influence of sin in his life. Sin can no longer have any power over him. So believers who are now related to Christ in and through his death, are to reckon or count themselves dead to sin. We are 'released from sin' – provision has been made for us to live a Christlike life. Peter has already stated this clearly in 2:24: 'He himself bore our sins in his body on the tree *so that we might die to sins and live for righteousness.'* This is the view we are now to take. As the death of Christ finished his involvement with sin, so our identification with him in his death means an entirely new attitude to sin in *our* lives. That change of attitude brought about by a change of heart, will in turn produce a change of direction.

In the previous chapter Peter had written about baptism and its value in symbolising that change (3:21). This instruction from Peter is very similar to Paul's teaching on being dead to sin and alive in Christ (Rom. 6:8-12) and Charles Wesley expressed similar truths and his own personal testimony in these tremendous words:

> Long my imprisoned spirit lay
> Fast bound in sin and nature's night;
> Thine eye diffused a quickening ray,
> I woke, the dungeon flamed with light;
> My chains fell off, my heart was free,
> I rose, went forth, and followed Thee.

As a result, he does not live the rest of his earthly life for evil human desires, but rather for the will of God (v. 2). Here is the contrast. The death of Christ for the believer has secured the death of the believer to the world. He would now rather live for the will of God.

Stibbs draws attention to the contrast between 'evil human desires' (AV, lusts of men) and the 'will of God'. They are two plural nouns set against two single nouns. 'The Christian life if rightly ordered, can enjoy a unity and an integration impossible to sinners. For there is only one true God; and for His people He has at any one time only one will. By contrast sinners are distracted and pulled first one way and then that by desire to satisfy the varied appetites which dominate those in whose company they find themselves.'[3]

The Greek word *pauo* means to stop or cease, but it is used at the end of the first verse in a passive and not an active sense. Peter is not suggesting that the believer cannot sin,

but that he is no longer dominated by sin; he is no longer a
slave of sin. The believer now finds that he has resources
which were not available to him previously. Christ's work
for him and in him, has made provision for him to be free to
serve God and do his will. Dr. Vernon McGee illustrates this
from the story of the prodigal son (Luke 15:11-32). He
reminds us that though the prodigal got down into the pigpen,
he wasn't a pig. He had the nature of his father who lived in
a mansion. Because of that he didn't like eating swill from a
trough. He enjoyed sitting down at a table covered with a
cloth and eating with tools. He liked good food and drink.
'Peter says that you are now identified with Christ. When
you came to the Lord Jesus you were born again.... My friend,
you *cannot* be a child of God and go out and live in the pigpen.
Let's face it – if you do, you are a pig. Pigs live in pigpens
and they love it, but sons do not love the pigpen.'[4] Such had
been the experience of some of those to whom Peter wrote.

**For you have spent enough time in the past doing what
pagans choose to do – living in debauchery, lust, drunkenness, orgies, carousing and detestable idolatry (v. 3).**
Reference to pagans is usually understood to be non-Jews
and many of these practices were characteristics of pagan
worship. Hillyer helpfully categorizes these acts of immorality
into three groups: 'Sexual misconduct (debauchery, lust),
intemperance (drunkenness, orgies, carousing), and
misdirected worship (detestable idolatry). The last would
often have involved all the other malpractices.'[5]

The word **detestable** means illegal, and is translated as
'lawless' in the RSV indicating that some of these activities
were actually forbidden by the law. They were practices
which, as Barclay says, 'outrage common decency'.

The time which any one person spends on this earth is
very limited in comparison to the infinity of eternity.
Therefore with such restricted time available to them, and as
God's creatures, they should not have spent *any* of it involved
in such things. So Peter tells them that enough time has already

been wasted. In 1:18 he had already referred to it as an **empty way of life** but now they have Christ to fill that void.

Though we may not have been involved in the specific practices listed here we were still sinners, disobedient to God, and still characterised by an empty way of life from which Christ died to deliver us. In fact any selfish ambitions however legitimate they may appear to be, are characteristics of self and therefore sinful in that they cut across the will of God for my life. Every one of us 'has turned to his own way' (Isa. 53:6) the essential characteristic of sin. The cross changes that because its underlying message is crystal clear – 'not my will, but yours be done' (Luke 22:42). 'Your will be done on earth' is an essential part of the Disciples' Prayer (Matt. 6:10).

As Christians these believers should not use **the rest of** (their) **earthly life** doing those things which were characteristics of their former life. Stuart Briscoe points out that Peter refers to what the 'pagans *choose* to do.' He says: 'If pagans can choose to do things, converted pagans can choose not to do them.'[6] There are after all only two alternatives. We either do **the will of God** or **what pagans choose to do**. Our decision will determine to which camp we belong.

Remember, these believers have 'tasted that the Lord is good' (2:3) and they now realise that his *will* for them is good (see Romans 12:2). What possible reason could they have for reverting to their old ways?

But others will not understand says Peter. **They think it strange that you do not plunge with them in to the same flood of dissipation, and they heap abuse on you (v. 4).** It genuinely surprises unbelievers that Christians have no desire to join in, and they abuse them for it; they literally 'blaspheme' them. Though the word is more often used of profanity in regard to God, it can be used of the vilification of God's people. In many parts of the world today you can profess the Christian faith without too much inconvenience, so long as you are prepared to join them in their reckless pursuits. There is such a variety of beliefs that they have no problem in accommodating yours, that is until you opt out by saying, 'That's not for me – I'm drawing a line at that.' Notice then how the atmosphere changes. As a general principle, either we are going to please God or we shall please men. If we please men, we will, almost certainly, make it our practice to not please God. This is due partly to the fact that the world doesn't understand, and any of us are suspicious of something or someone who is different. But their antagonism is more likely because our lifestyle makes them uncomfortable.

What a perverse and peculiar world we live in. If an individual because of a dissolute life causes harm to himself and disruption to his family, the world may not take too much notice. If on the other hand he stops drinking and lives a pure life many think he has gone mad! But that puts him in very good company (Mark 3:21)!

Nowhere does Scripture teach that the believer should be an isolationist. The isolation ward in a hospital provides for exclusion and that is not the New Testament pattern for the Christian. Our Lord was not an isolationist – he was very much *in* the world, as we are to be. But he was clearly different *to* the world; he was separate *from*, other than the world, and in that he is a perfect pattern for those who profess to follow him. He was 'done with sin', and we are to be done with it as well. So the New Testament underlines the necessity of separation in the life of every believer. Christ has closed yesterday's door; things are different now.

And if others judge us now because they don't understand, we should remember that a day is coming when God will judge them: **But they will have to give account to him who is ready to judge the living and the dead (v. 5)**. No one escapes their ultimate accountability to God. Even physical death does not provide escape from judgment. God is **ready** to judge; that is it is part of his character to do this, and he is prepared for it. That judgment will certainly be made because of their rejection of God but it will also include judgment of their treatment of believers.

The Day of Judgment is signalled by the return of Christ. When he comes there will be both **the living and the dead**; that is those still living and those who have previously died. And within both the living and the dead there will be those who are *spiritually* alive and those who are *spiritually* dead. Those who are spiritually alive through trusting in the merits of Christ's cross have nothing to fear at this judgment, for the judge appointed by God is Jesus Christ himself (John 5:22; Acts 10:42; 17:31). Because it is a function attributed to Christ, this phrase later found its way into the creeds of the Christian church, e.g., 'he shall come to judge the quick and the dead.'

Christians do have a judgment to face but since their sins have already been forgiven it is not a judgment to condemnation (Rom. 8:1). It is a judgment of works following conversion and to assess rewards (2 Cor. 5:10, see also Matthew 25).

However those who do not accept Christ as Saviour will face him as Judge. Jesus warned that there would be those who could offer some of the best credentials but that 'on that day' he would have to say to them, 'I never knew you. Away from me you evildoers' (Matt. 7:23)! Never has the human ear heard such dreadful words. It is the cross and its appeal that Peter has been writing about, and if the cross is rejected then there is no other antidote for sin. Almost no judgment today appears to be final. There always seems to be a higher court to which we can appeal. But not for those who hear the judgment words from Christ. His is the final word.

It is therefore important that those who understand the message of the cross, should live out the practicalities of that message in order that others might see and believe, even if there are those who will not understand. Part of their reaction stems from envy, and that in itself might be a means to an end. Chuck Swindoll puts it like this: 'Let's not forget that God has left us here on purpose. We're here to demonstrate what it is like to be a member of another country, to have citizenship in another land, so that we might create a desire for others to emigrate.'[7]

There will be times when we must speak, but there will be even more occasions when our lives will be the challenge to their lifestyle. Blasphemy will offend us but as Swindoll says: 'you cannot clean up anybody's lips until you've cleaned up his or her heart. And ultimately that's Christ's job.' What we are seeing and hearing in their lives are the signs of being spiritually lost, and so we must be sure that the contrast in our lives is clearly visible.

Peter continues to expand on what will happen at judgment: **For this is the reason the gospel was preached even to those who are now dead, so that they might be judged in regard to the body, but live according to God in regard to the spirit (v. 6).** Some have advocated that this must suggest a second opportunity to respond to the gospel after death. The context here and the Scriptures as a whole cannot support that view. Peter is writing of those who had the gospel preached to them but are 'now dead', that is at the time he wrote the words.

Almost certainly this verse has no link with the passage in the previous chapter where Christ 'preached to the spirits in prison' (v. 19). There the word *keryssein* is used which means 'to proclaim.' Here (and in 1:12,25) Peter uses the word *euangelizesthai* meaning 'to preach good news'. This is the more usual word for the preaching of the gospel.

This refers to those who heard the gospel, responded positively, but have since died physically. They as men have been judged as sinners and this has been dealt with by Christ, whereas in the spirit both here and hereafter they enjoy life in all its fulness.

These words serve as an encouragement to believers in the first century who had concerns about those who died prior to Christ's return. Paul also deals with the same issue (1 Thess. 4:13-18).

Peter's readers need have no fear that the righteous judge

will vindicate those who put their trust in him, whatever the judgment of men on them might be. As Horatius Bonar has expressed it:

> Go, labour on; 'tis not for naught;
> Thy earthly loss is heavenly gain;
> Men heed thee, love thee, praise thee not;
> The Master praises – what are men?

Just before his appearance before the Council of Constance in 1414 Jan Hus, the Reformer who was martyred for his faith, wrote to one of his friends:

> I shall not be led astray by them to the side of evil, though I suffer at His will temptations, revilings, imprisonments, and deaths – as indeed He too suffered, and hath subjected His loved servants to the same trials, leaving us an example that we may suffer for His sake and our salvation. If He suffered, being what He was, why should not we?[8]

2. SERVICE (verses 7-11)

Peter tells these believers that **the end of all things is near (v. 7)**. The **end of all things** is always to be regarded as imminent but this may not only refer to the consummation of the world but also to each individual life. Everything that makes up our present age is so transient. It is natural to be taken up with the things of this world and to act as if we will be here for ever. That attitude gets adjusted when through sober thinking or perhaps the introduction of tragedy we discover that time is limited. Perhaps a member of our family or a friend has been told that due to illness their time on this earth is to be shorter than they thought. Suddenly there are different priorities. Ordinary events take on a new meaning and so much that took up their time previously becomes less important. Many situations in life prove the truth of Peter's statement.

A few years ago I was crossing a road in Miami. It was the first day of my stay there and I hadn't adjusted to the traffic flow on the right side of the road. I was dodging between lines of cars stopped at traffic lights and looked the wrong way. A truck travelling very fast in the other lane avoided me by centimetres. My heart still misses a beat as I realise how near I was to the end of my earthly life.

Certainly the circumstances which both Peter and his readers found themselves in would make his comment extremely relevant. We do not know when **the end of all things** for us might be. Peter probably realises that he cannot expect his own life to last much longer. Who knows what Nero might do next. Though Peter's words have an ominous ring to them, they are to be regarded more as a source of encouragement than a warning.

So what do Christians do when confronted with the uncertainty and brevity of life. They don't panic – they pray. **Therefore be clear minded and self controlled so that you can pray.**

The **therefore** introduces a list of Peter's priorities for those who are living when **the end of all things is near**. All kinds of dangers and uncertainties can lead to over excitement so we should be careful not to lose our mental balance. Today's generation might say 'Stay cool', Peter says **be clear minded**, don't panic, remember that God is in control.

We should also be **self controlled**, that is, 'sober' or calm. We should maintain a balanced approach. Clowney uses the phrase 'realistic living'. Some adopt an extreme view when faced with the end times. One writer refers to those who 'give way to eschatological frenzy'. One saint when asked what alteration he would make to his plans if he knew that his life was to end or that Christ was to come in the next hour, replied that he would not make any changes but continue just as he had intended. This was not a contrived and overly pious response, but a humble acknowledgment that he was endeavouring to serve God moment by moment, and could do no more. The hope of Christ's return *one day* should be enough to keep us faithful in the duties of *this day*.

Stuart Briscoe tells the story of the astronaut bound for the moon who was asked, 'How will you get off the moon?' He replied, 'We fire rockets and we take off in our little module.' 'But what happens if it doesn't fire?' He said, 'Then we're stuck.' 'How long will your life-support system last?' 'Six hours.' The reporter then asked, 'May I ask you what you will do for the last six hours?' 'Sure,' he said. 'I'll work on the engine!'[9]

When we are living in the end times we continue to do what we have been doing, calmly and with sound judgment. If the Lord interrupts that, so be it, and if that is by his return that will be wonderful, but until then, we go on day by day as if we were going to see our earthly life through. As Briscoe says, 'The believer in tune with him simply keeps on fixing the engine.'

And says Peter, both of these qualities will equip us to pray. The idea of being self controlled and alert is the opposite to being drunk or asleep. Peter remembered that he failed to pray in Gethsemane because he fell asleep and he was spiritually the weaker for it. In contrast the Lord had felt the necessity of prayer and was the stronger for it. But effective prayer does not have to be lengthy. Michael Bentley remarks on the fact that he was encouraged when he learnt of the fact that 'the godly C H Spurgeon never prayed for more than ten minutes at a time because he had a problem over concentration. He found it much better to pray in short snatches, but often. Why do we keep listening to Satan who tells us that God will only listen to long, well rounded phrases which are full of deep thoughts.'[10]

Then having got the vertical relationship right, look to the horizontal. **Above all, love each other deeply (v. 8)**. By using the phrase **Above all** meaning 'before everything else', Peter indicates the supremacy of love. So much else in our Christian lives depends on its presence. It reflects the Commandments

given by God, which Jesus underlined in such a
comprehensive way. ' "Love the Lord your God with all your
heart and with all your soul and with all your mind." This is
the first and greatest commandment. And the second is like
it: "Love your neighbour as yourself." All the Law and the
Prophets hang on these two commandments' (Matt. 22:37 -
40). The whole of our religion is summed up firstly in a love
for God which then results in a love for our fellow man.
Nothing is a better witness than when believers express
Christian love for each other. Nothing is a poorer witness
when they don't.

Therefore since this is the evidence of our faith and the
'badge of discipleship' (John 13:35), the existence of love
between Christians is assumed (1:22). Peter now calls for a
stretching of that. It is the word *ektenos*, translated 'fervent'
or 'constant', which can imply stretching, as with a horse at
full gallop or an athlete reaching for the tape. That requires
effort and so does this kind of love. Wiersbe confirms a belief
I have and have expressed, but which I think has prompted
some misunderstanding! 'It is even possible to love people
that we do not like!' because he says 'It is not a matter of
emotional feeling, though that is included, but of dedicated
will. Christian love means that we treat others the way God
treats us...'[11]

And this special love will be ready to forgive time and
time again **because love covers over a multitude of sins**.
Peter probably has in mind Proverbs 10:12: 'Hatred stirs up
dissensions but love covers all wrongs.' Nowhere does the
Scripture ever suggest that love can condone sin. God, even
with the greatness of his love, never does that. What we learn
here is that this 'stretched love' covers sin. We can overlook
a fellow believer's irritating habits, and this love will forgive
others who have hurt us, and as often as necessary. Certainly,
a Christian should never broadcast another believer's failure
for all the world to hear. Gossip causes much unnecessary
pain in the church, and much harm to the faith outside of it.

Another virtue which is commended in view of 'the end of all things' is hospitality: **Offer hospitality to one another without grumbling (v. 9)**. Rejected by the mainstream religions, the Christian church in the first century often had to meet in homes. In addition those embracing the Christian faith often found themselves ostracised, even thrown out by their families. It was important that love expressed itself in giving hospitality to them.

Through thirty years of ministry I have cause to be grateful to God for believers who have opened their homes for a weary itinerant evangelist. Thank God for those who are 'given to hospitality'. But it does not only have to be for the benefit of an evangelist or a missionary. There are those in every church who because of their circumstances would appreciate an offer of hospitality. As we share Sunday lunch with our families, remember that there are many who go home to an empty house. Wives of itinerant preachers sometimes spend days alone because of their husband's absence. Some of our brothers and sisters in Christ spend Christmas and Easter on their own. Then there are some who see no one from one Sunday to the next, and would appreciate an invitation to our home.

And what about using our home as an evangelistic tool? Many who would not darken the door of a church would come into our homes where we may have the opportunity of sharing our faith with them. Remember that much of first century evangelism was from 'house to house' and much of the Lord's ministry was exercised in the informal situation. Many Christians have experienced a special blessing from God as they have been able to **offer hospitality** in different ways.

Peter adds too, that we should never grumble at the time and expense required in doing this. Hillyer quotes Donald Coggan, former Archbishop of Canterbury, who said: 'True Christian hospitality is making people feel at home, when you wish they were at home.'[12] But I think that Peter meant a little more than that! Invariably there is a cost to this ministry, both in monetary terms and in the sacrifice of our privacy and our 'free time.'

And our homes are not the only gifts we have received from God.

Each one should use whatever gift he has received to serve others, faithfully administering God's grace in its various forms (v. 10). Every believer has some gift or gifts which can be used for the benefit of the community. Peter uses the word *charisma* which indicates that he is referring to a gift from God, though he does not specifically refer to the Holy Spirit. This gift is not given to the Christian for his own benefit or to pander to his pride, but in order that he might serve others, thus making him a steward or trustee of that gift. Every blessing received from God is totally undeserved; it is of his grace. Our privilege is to administer God's grace to others in its various forms, and to do it **faithfully**, literally 'as good managers'. Emphasis has often been made of the fact that as we serve God we may not always see the results we would like or even expect to see, but that our fundamental responsibility is to do what we do **faithfully**.

In the story which Jesus told, each servant was entrusted with talents by his master 'according to his ability'. Some had more than others but all those who had been obedient received the same commendation; 'Well done, good and *faithful* servant' (Matt. 25:14-30). My heart should ask, 'Will he say that to me?'

Then Peter makes reference to a special gift from God: **If anyone speaks, he should do it as one speaking the very words of God. If anyone serves, he should do it with the strength God provides (v. 11).** Two ministries are mentioned in this verse which cover speaking and doing.

Whilst all believers are to be ready to give an answer for the hope that they have, Peter refers here to proclaiming the 'oracles' of God (RSV); a reference to the preaching of the gospel. Not everyone has the privilege and responsibility of preaching or teaching. Those who do should speak words as spoken by God himself, that is, all that he says should accord with the teaching of Scripture. If a man is not **speaking the very words of God**, he has no business standing in the pulpit.

To preach the word of God was certainly a characteristic of every servant of God in the Bible. Paul was able to say to the converts in Thessalonica: 'When you received the word of God, which you heard from us, you accepted it not as the word of men, but as it actually is, the word of God' (1 Thess. 2:13). To the Corinthians he says that he and his fellow workers are 'Christ's ambassadors, as though God were making his appeal through us. We implore you on Christ's behalf. Be reconciled to God' (2 Cor. 5:20).

Paul was called by God, as was Peter, to speak for God in this particular way. Only those called and gifted by God would dare to accept such an awesome and daunting task, and they in turn look to the prayerful support of others (Col. 4:3-4).

The other ministry mentioned is that of service. The word for **serves** covers a wide variety of opportunities to serve others. There is no definitive list in the New Testament. Paul gives some examples (as in 1 Corinthians 12:27-31) but Peter doesn't even attempt that. Our gifts will be varied and although we may be able to identify the ones that are most obvious, we may not find the limit of our capabilities until we begin to serve. They are often best identified 'warm', that is when we are actually serving, rather than by a 'cold' intellectual approach. That gift or gifts might prove to be a 'backroom job' but in God's eyes equally important in the life of the church (see again 1 Corinthians 12:14-26).

But it does not matter whether the task is preaching the gospel or cleaning the church, it is to be done **with the strength which God provides**. God supplies enough strength to do his will. There is no commendation in the Scriptures for taking on every task we can see or even those that we can see *need* to be done! That is not the image conveyed by Paul's picture of the church being a body with every component having its own part to play.

I remember hearing someone say, 'The pathway of
Christian service is strewn with nervous wrecks; never the
pathway of obedience.' We should remember that God
provides all that we need to do his will – not more or less.

So why should we be clear minded and pray? Why should
we love one another at full stretch? Why should we offer
hospitality? Why should we serve each other? Peter says **so
that in all things God may be praised through Jesus Christ**.
Here is the intended goal of all Christian service, that as God's
gifts are put to the benefit of others and done in his strength,
he is praised. There can be no greater motive than that.

Do we understand from this that the praise goes to God or
to Christ? Since Peter suggests that the praise is **through
Jesus Christ** either could be true.

On some occasions when 'gifts' are discussed today it can
produce strife, maybe because it is done with a spirit of self
promotion. Peter's emphasis here makes it clear that all gifts
are bestowed for the ultimate benefit of others not for self
gratification and so the praise rightly goes to the Giver.

**To him be the glory and the power for ever and ever.
Amen**. When Paul considered the grace of God it was
common for him to add a similar doxology (2 Cor. 11:31;
Gal. 1:5; Eph. 3:21; Phil. 4:20; 1 Tim. 6:16). What a difference
it would make to our service if we always did everything for
the glory of God. Chuck Swindoll asks: 'How many church
conflicts could be resolved if God's glory were everybody's
goal? How many egos would be put in their place if God's
glory – not human glory – were at stake? How much
extremism would be avoided if we did all for the greater glory
of God?'[13]

Stibbs suggests that this is better read as a statement than
a prayer: 'Whose is the glory and the dominion' with 'Amen'
serving as the endorsement – 'so it is' rather than as a request
'so be it'.[14] If the one referred to is Christ, it is a clear
confirmation of his deity.

These verses have helped us to understand how we can

use the rest of our earthly lives **for the will of God** and
especially in view of the fact that **the end of all things is
near**.

3. SUFFERING (verses 12-19)

Peter now addresses the specific **painful trial** which his
readers are about to face. This is to be something different to
the 'everyday' persecution which is promised as the lot of
'everyone who wants to live a godly life in Christ Jesus' (2
Tim. 3:12). The years that lay ahead would produce successive
emperors who would persecute the Christian church. This
then was to be official persecution from the state. Until that
point in time Christians had been tolerated as a section of
Judaism, which had always been acceptable to the Romans.
Now things were going to be different.

The suffering which Peter addresses here is unique because
it is suffering directly due to the fact of being a Christian:
**Dear friends, do not be surprised at the painful trial you
are suffering as though something strange were happening
to you (v. 12). Dear friends** is sometimes translated
'Beloved'. Peter is speaking of that which is unique to
believers. If you are a Christian this is something that has
your name on it.

Christians must understand that the suffering they
experience is not mischance. That cannot happen to the
children of a Sovereign God. The word **happening** means
'to go together', indicating that it is not an accident; therefore
Peter's readers must not view it with surprise or shame.

In fact a quick survey of history would show them that it
would be the *absence* of persecution which would be more
surprising! Through the centuries those who have lived
righteous lives have inevitably suffered because of it. The
world doesn't usually object to what it comprehends as
'religion' but it cannot stand righteousness. Amazingly in
some cases the 'religious' have been leading the attack! It
was those in that position who schemed to have Christ killed.

The Scripture also points out that **the painful trial** is God-appointed, and therefore with the divine purpose to test and purify faith (see again 3:17). God is in perfect control of the situation, and has begun his refining work in the lives of his new creations. Swindoll suggests that as Christians we belong to God's schoolroom and in every school there have to be tests to gauge progress. But says Swindoll: 'The wonderful thing about God's schoolroom, however, is that we get to grade our own papers. You see, He doesn't test us so He can learn how well we're doing. He tests us so *we* can discover how well we're doing.'[15] Perhaps in a test we had ten years ago we didn't show up too well, but a more recent one which was even tougher suggests that we have matured from where we were.

The Apostle James wrote along similar lines when he said: 'Consider it pure joy, my brothers, whenever you face trials of many kinds, because you know that the testing of your faith develops perseverance. Perseverance must finish its work so that you may be mature and complete, not lacking anything' (James 1:2-4). James is quite clear that it will happen – 'whenever you face trials' not 'if ever' you do – and that God has a wonderful purpose in it all, so we must persevere.

The translation 'fiery trial', used in the Authorised Version, is certainly a reference to the process used in refining metals (see 1:7). This phrase again underlines the fact that Peter is not referring here to general suffering, and certainly not that pain which through disobedience we bring on ourselves. This trial comes solely because we stand faithfully for God as we bear the name of Christ.

How tenderly Peter needs to address this question. He has endeavoured to remind them how privileged and secure they are and what a tremendous hope they have, now he has to inform them of the realities of living the Christian life in a pagan world. For Gentile believers in particular this would be an extremely difficult concept to grasp. To suffer for religion would appear incongruous and would not seem to fit in with the blessings of the gospel. If he is able to convince them that this is not something which should surprise them, then not only can it be accepted, it can also be a means of rejoicing!

But rejoice that you participate in the sufferings of Christ, so that you may be overjoyed when his glory is revealed (v. 13). Peter does not suggest that any kind of suffering should cause them to rejoice. They are to rejoice because they are identified with Christ. In his life and in his death he participated in the world's suffering. Trials for the believer will provide a glimpse into that suffering which Christ experienced, and will also bring him into a more intimate fellowship with his Lord as he shares in his suffering.

When people persecute the believer they are in fact persecuting Christ. Following his persecution of believers, Saul of Tarsus was challenged by the Lord 'Why do you persecute *me*?' (Acts 9:4). Clowney writes: 'We partake of his sufferings, not by contributing to his atonement, but by following in his steps (2:21).'[16] This was part of Paul's great ambition (see Philippians 3:10). Trials therefore serve this greater purpose of bringing us closer to the Lord, and this in itself, says Peter, should cause us to rejoice.

Acts records the occasion when Peter and the other apostles were beaten and ordered to stop preaching in the name of Jesus. What did they do? 'The apostles left the Sanhedrin, rejoicing because they had been counted worthy of suffering disgrace *for the Name*. Day after day, in the temple courts and from house to house, they never stopped teaching and proclaiming the good news that Jesus is the Christ' (Acts 5: 41-42). They rejoiced because they 'had been *counted worthy* of suffering'. Peter wants to convey this idea of privilege to his readers.

And there is more! Just as hard and laborious work is often translated into success, and just as the athlete's long and sometimes painful effort is translated into victory, so Scripture teaches that suffering is translated into glory. Paul writes of believers sharing in Christ's sufferings '*in order that* we may also share in his glory' (Rom. 8:17).

So their joy will not be just for the present. Peter underlines his great theme of hope. There will be even greater joy in that day when Christ's glory is revealed and everyone acknowledges him as Lord. The prospect of having a share in this (1:7, 8; 5:1) should cause them to rejoice even more. The Greek term *charete agalliomenoi* speaks of an overflowing joy which will fill every believing heart at that time.

In the early days of Christianity 'the single word *name* was synonymous with the Christian religion.'[17] So Peter writes: **If you are insulted because of the name of Christ, you are blessed**. These words echo the words of Jesus himself: 'Blessed are you when people insult you, and persecute you and falsely say all kinds of evil against you because of me. Rejoice and be glad, because great is your reward in heaven' (Matt. 5:11,12).

The insults come because we are associated with Jesus, the Son of God. That has to be a privilege not a misfortune. Peter is referring to something more than a few harsh words. This is more like character assassination. Such was the antagonism between the church and society that when a Christian out of conscience opted out 'this led not merely to misunderstanding and resentment by uncomprehending pagan neighbours; it could readily be interpreted as antisocial at best or treasonable at worst.'[18] The word **'blessed'** contains the idea of contentment or being 'filled full', which is experienced because the Spirit of God is with us.

The second phrase – **for the Spirit of glory and of God rests on you** – refers to the Holy Spirit and appears in Isaiah (11:2). Jesus used it of himself in the synagogue (Luke 4:18) and now Peter applies it with amplification to suffering believers. These people know a special anointing of the Holy Spirit. Isn't this one of the reasons why those who suffer and even die for their faith often do so with joy?

The amplification is the addition of the reference to **glory**.

The *Shekinah* was the manifestation of the glory of the Lord in the Old Testament and the reminder to the people of God's presence with them. Here in the New Testament God's people are equally assured of his presence with them.

What a blessing, says Peter, that the evidence of Christ's presence with us, even in us, is the fact that we suffer because of our association with him.

For this reason, it is important that believers don't bring suffering upon themselves: **If you suffer, it should not be as a murderer or thief or any other kind of criminal, or even as a meddler (v. 15).** The references to murder and stealing seem extreme for a Christian. Perhaps Peter mentions these because they carried the death penalty which would be the ultimate fate of those convicted for their Christian witness. Therefore to suffer for the other reasons would undermine the witness of Christian suffering.

Peter also says that they should not suffer **as a meddler** or as 'a busybody in other men's matters' (AV). The Greek word *allotriepiskopos* means literally 'to be watching over other people's affairs'. There is sometimes the idea presented that Christians should have the right to meddle in the affairs of others. They believe that everyone they come across is under their own personal jurisdiction, whereas it is sometimes better to leave these matters for God's judgment. There is nothing 'spiritual' about being hurt because we interfered in something that was not our business. Then and now, this kind of person makes Christianity unnecessarily unpopular among unbelievers and subsequently spoils the witness.

These things are sin, and Peter tells them that they should never be suffering for their own sin, since God never tests us with sin. James confirms this when he writes: 'When tempted, no one should say, "God is tempting me." For God cannot be tempted by evil, nor does he tempt anyone' (James 1:13).

However, if you suffer as a Christian, do not be ashamed (v. 16). This is one of the few occasions when the word 'Christian' is used in the Bible. It was first used in

Antioch when it was popularised as a nickname for believers (Acts 11:26). It became a term of derision; a vulgar word. Agrippa was scornful of it when speaking to Paul (Acts 26:28). It was said, 'Well bred people avoided pronouncing the name or when forced to do so made a kind of apology.'

In much of today's society the term 'Christian' is not understood as it was in those days. It does not prompt immediate antagonism because in the minds of many the word equates with respectability or, alternatively, refers to an aspect of their nationality. In truth the term has become devalued. It is when it becomes clear just what a biblical Christian is, that the embers of persecution will begin to glow. Most today will have little objection to references to Christianity *as they perceive it*, or to activities within our denomination or church. Only when we speak directly of our identification with Christ and the demands that makes on us will problems begin to arise.

There was no such confusion in the first century and Peter uses the term very deliberately here. He says there is no cause for shame in having to suffer for his name's sake, indeed he says **praise God that you bear that name**. It is a cause of thankfulness because firstly they have this evidence that they are Christians and secondly they can look forward to the advantages that come from that suffering even as Christ did.

Then follows the sting! And what an important reminder this is for those of us who can become so wrapped up in our comfortable Christianity that we forget God's judgment: **For it is time for judgment to begin with the family of God (v. 17)**. It is thought that this is a reference to some fearful trial which might shortly arrive for believers. Certainly the reference is in particular to the church of God, literally 'the household' or temple. Peter has this latter idea in mind (2:4-5).

The Bible clearly shows that God's people in every generation have suffered; it is not an option, it is a necessity. It is the prerequisite to Christlikeness. God invariably deals with the testing and purification of his own first of all (Jer. 25:29; 49:12; Ezek. 9:6; Mal. 3:1-5).

Clowney remarks: 'Fiery trials are not easily endured, but testing does not destroy us, it saves us.'[19] Most Christians can point to some experience in their life which though painful at the time taught them a lesson which they needed to learn, and produced a little more of the likeness of Christ in them. And if this process has meant pain and loss even for those who are justified, what will be the end of the ungodly? If God does not spare his own people, then he will certainly not spare others.

And if it begins with us, what will the outcome be for those who do not obey the gospel of God? Notice that Peter includes himself. Though he is writing to those over a large area, the warning is for all. This is not to be an isolated, local persecution.

The ultimate judgment is for **those who do not obey the gospel**, that is, those who reject the gospel and persecute its followers. God commands all men everywhere to repent (Acts 17:30). To refuse to do so, is to reject a divine order which will initiate a divine judgment which is too terrible to contemplate (Rev. 20:10-15).

And 'If it is hard for the righteous to be saved, what will become of the ungodly and the sinner?' (v. 18). This is a quotation from the Septuagint (Prov. 11:31). The word **hard** is also translated 'difficult' or even 'scarcely' in other places. This is not to imply that it is difficult for God to save us or that there is any doubt about our ultimate salvation, though it must be said that what God did was no easy thing. I remember a preacher once suggesting that creation was an easier task for God since he only had to speak and it was done. There was indeed a much greater cost involved in bringing about the new creation!

The righteous will be saved, but it will not be easy, Peter tells us. While recognising God's sovereign power in fulfilling his purposes in our lives, there is truth in the fact that we do not make it easy for him. Wiersbe shows us that Lot is a good Old Testament illustration of this fact. It was not difficult for God to rescue Lot from Sodom but Lot made it more difficult that it need have been because of his unwillingness. He was eventually saved but 'only as one escaping through the flames (1 Cor. 3:9-15).'[20]

John Wesley referred to himself as 'a brand plucked from the burning' and that is true of many of us.

So, **If it is hard for the righteous to be saved, what will become of the ungodly and the sinner?** Peter doesn't answer the question, since the answer is obvious. They will certainly perish; there is no hope. If the righteous are saved with such difficulty, then the unrighteous will not be saved at all. Therefore a Christian should never be tempted to seek vengeance for himself, even if he has been harshly persecuted. We are in the privileged position we enjoy, only by the grace of God, and this promise of the consuming flames reserved for the unrighteous should rather be a spur to each believer to use every opportunity while there is time, to share the good news through our lives and with our lips.

And as to the Christian's own position? **So then, those who suffer according to God's will should commit themselves to their faithful Creator and continue to do good (v. 19)**. Christians must acknowledge that they suffer according to God's will; he is their **Creator** and thus the controller of life. This is the only occasion in the New Testament where God is referred to in this way. He is the one who is responsible for the whole of creation, indeed the very hairs of their head are numbered. He knows the purpose behind their suffering, and because he is **faithful** and always keeps his promises, he can be trusted. They should have no anxiety in committing themselves to him. The usual temptation is to face a problem by relying at least first of all in our own resources. Wrong! We have a faithful Creator to whom we can commit ourselves.

Commit is a technical term for depositing a deed or sum of money or other valuable with anyone in trust. So says Peter, they should view their life as a deposit; lay it confidently in his hands, and they will surely find him faithful to what a Creator ought to be. Does Peter have in mind our Lord's final words on the cross? 'Father, into your hands I commit my spirit' (Luke 23:46). He certainly uses the same word.

Meanwhile the responsibility of his readers is **to do good**. This was and always will be our business. Whatever men do to us, or say to us, we give evidence of our commitment to God by continuing **to do good**.

Men and women engaged in that mission can safely entrust their interests to God.

References

1. Stuart Briscoe, *Holy Living in a Hostile World*, Harold Shaw, 1982, p. 157.
2. Edmund P Clowney, *The Message of 1 Peter*, IVP, 1988, p. 169.
3. A. M. Stibbs, *I Peter*, Tyndale Commentaries, 1959, p. 149.
4. Vernon McGee, *Thru the Bible Commentary Series*, 1 Peter, Thomas Nelson, 1991, p. 81.
5. N. Hillyer, *I Peter*, New International Biblical Commentary, Paternoster, 1992, p. 121.
6. Briscoe, p. 161.
7. Chuck Swindoll, *Hope Again*, Word, 1996, p. 167.
8. Quoted in John Moffatt, *The General Epistles*, Hodder & Stoughton, 1928, p. 147.
9. Briscoe, p. 169.
10. Michael Bentley, *Living for God in a Pagan World*, Evangelical Press, 1990, p. 148.
11. Warren Wiersbe, *Be Hopeful*, Victor Books, 1982, p. 117.
12. Hillyer, p. 126.
13. Swindoll, p. 194.
14. Stibbs, p. 157.
15. Swindoll, p. 204.
16. Clowney, p. 191.
17. Simon Kistemaker, quoted by Michael Bentley.
18. Hillyer, p. 131.
19. Clowney, p. 195.
20. Wiersbe, p. 129.

CHAPTER
FIVE

SOMETHING
FOR
EVERYONE

Peter moves toward the end of his letter by sharing a personal word with those in positions of leadership in the church. In the light of the pressure which they are going to face, he realises that things must be right from the top. Graciously and humbly and from his own experience, some of it painful, he addresses those to whom the rest of the church will look for example.

But what if you are not a leader? Don't switch off! God's Word will have something to say to you from these verses.

1. AN APPEAL TO OUR ELDERS (verses 1-4)

Some of the best attested texts have the word 'therefore' in the opening phrase of this chapter. If this was in the mind of the writer then it provides a link with what has gone before, and in particular to the references of God's judgment. Peter now presents a solemn charge to those who share the responsibility of office within the church: **To the elders among you, I appeal as a fellow elder, a witness of Christ's sufferings and one who also will share in the glory to be revealed (v. 1).**

Elders, as prominent members of the church, would perhaps be more liable to God's judgment since more would be expected of them. Beside that, believers suffering persecution would look to the elders for leadership and example.

The word 'elder' (*presbuteros*) means properly 'one who is old', but it is frequently used in the New Testament of officers of the church. Only one office is mentioned here, though other verses in the New Testament indicate that in addition, local churches appointed deacons for specific tasks (Acts 6:1-6; 1 Tim. 3:8-13). Other terms used in the early church such as bishops (overseers) and pastors (shepherds) were alternative references to elders, being more descriptive of their responsibilities.

Since the word for **elder** in the original does not in this instance have the definite article with it, it is just possible that the reference includes all who are senior members of the

145

church (in contrast to the young in verse 5) and therefore have some share in looking after the various fellowships, but the content of Peter's exhortations seems to be directed mainly to those who hold office in the church.

Notice the sensitive way in which Peter addresses them: **I appeal**. This is not issued as a command but includes the idea of encouragement, entreaty, and exhortation. Peter does not 'wave the big stick' though his authority as an apostle gave him that right (1:1). Rather he appeals **as a fellow elder**. There is a call in these verses to humble leadership and Peter sets the tone for this immediately. He expresses a sympathetic fellow feeling as one with similar responsibilities. He is a partner with them in the work.

He recognises too the potential temptations open to those holding this office. Pride is a great danger in the ministry and has been the downfall of many. Why should that be so? Think of the circumstances. Church leaders stand before groups of people and speak for God. Ministers are respected and trusted and rarely questioned. Many are virtually unaccountable. This is part and parcel of the privilege of leadership but it provides a minefield of dangers. We may begin to think we are infallible; that we alone know what is right. There may even be a measure of pride in what we have accomplished, though in truth we know that 'it is the Lord's doing.'

'If Peter, one of the original Twelve, the earliest spokesman for the church, an anointed servant of God, would not mention his role of importance, I think we can learn a lesson about humility. Mark it down. Don't forget it. The pride of position must be absent.'[1]

But though pride may be absent from Peter's heart, his position would surely be recognised by others. Ellicott refers to Peter as 'the head Christian of the world, and writing from the thick of persecution already in Rome, the Asiatic elders cannot set his advice down as that of some easy layman who is untouched by the difficulty.'[2] This is no uninformed observer.

He is also a **witness of Christ's sufferings**. The word for witness is not merely a spectator but one who gives testimony; one who proclaims what he has seen, though of course the first is necessary for the second. We can imagine the weight this carried. Peter is a guarantor of the truth that he preaches.

He could have referred to hearing the Lord's teaching ministry; to having seen his wonderful miracles, but he speaks of his death. Here was someone who almost certainly had seen the Saviour die. That time would also remind him of the lowest point in his life when he failed the Lord so miserably. But now he is restored to his service. He identifies with him in the closest possible way.

and one who also will share in the glory to be revealed. Stibbs suggests that there may be some link here to the transfiguration – perhaps Peter has in mind the fact that the transfiguration is a preview of Christ's glory as it will be revealed.[3]

In any case Peter implies that this is imminent since the phrase can be literally translated 'about to be revealed'. He is convinced, as supremely illustrated in Christ, that glory always follows suffering so that those who suffer with him will also reign with him. Peter anticipates a **share** in this – and soon. As he identifies with Christ in his suffering, so he will also share in his glory. Peter is looking forward to glory; part of the Christian's blessed hope.

Here is his first imperative to these leaders: **Be shepherds of God's flock that is under your care, serving as overseers – not because you must, but because you are willing, as God wants you to be; not greedy for money, but eager to serve (v. 2).** Peter gives to others the instruction which was given to him. At that early morning breakfast meeting Jesus had restored him after his denial, and then appointed him as a shepherd with the words, 'Take care of my sheep' (John 21:16).

To be a good spiritual shepherd you must be called and gifted by God. It is not something which can be easily learnt, primarily because it is a ministry of the heart. It is possible for a man to preach or teach effectively and yet not have the heart of a shepherd. There is no textbook or week long course of seminars which will make you a good shepherd. It has to be in the heart. If that is not the case then that man is not equipped to be a pastor, and the church will not grow under 'hirelings' (John 10:11-15).

I discovered this helpful description of a spiritual shepherd: 'By definition, the true elder is the shepherd of the flock in which God has placed him .... who bears them on his heart, seeks them when they stray, defends them from harm, comforts them in their pain, and feeds them with the truth.' This is particularly good because the verb used by Peter, *poimainein* meaning shepherd, or care for, suggests all that is involved in being a shepherd and not merely providing food. As well as the teaching of the Scriptures there will also be their tender application.

Wiersbe writes: 'The pastor is not a religious lecturer who weekly passes along information about the Bible. He is a shepherd who knows his people and seeks to help them through the Word.'[4] The spiritual shepherd is looking out for his people to see how they are doing. Paul's exhortation to the Ephesian elders was that they should '*keep watch over...* all the flock.... Be shepherds of the church of God' (Acts 20: 28).

The following references underline some of these various duties included in shepherding: caring (Isa. 40:11); feeding (John 21:15); guarding (Acts 20:29-30).

The picture of shepherding and sheep is common in the Scriptures and in both Old and New Testaments, and used in contrasting ways, though the other side of the coin is not particularly complimentary. It reminds us that we are the sheep with a proneness to go astray and a propensity to follow the crowd. Sheep seem to need looking after and protecting more than most other undomesticated animals. How providential that we have a 'Shepherd and Overseer' of our souls (2:25).

Peter indicates some of the characteristics of good shepherds or overseers. Each of them begins with a negative: *Not* **because you must...** *not* **greedy for money...** *not* **lording it over those entrusted to you**. Their service will be willing service as a true expression of Christian love. The shepherd serves because he *wants* to, not because he *has* to, indeed says Peter he is **eager to serve**. Again the emphasis is on his passion. His heart is in his work. And those who serve God in this way don't do it for material gain. Apparently there were (and still are) some who engaged in ministry for what they could make out of it.

God's servants should never be **greedy for money**. It is salutary that Paul also needs to add this qualification for elders and deacons in his letters (1 Tim. 3:8; Tit. 1:7). There are great temptations in this area and it has proved to be the downfall of many. Often the amount is not the major problem. It is possible to be a comparatively poor minister and yet be motivated by money. Anyone who performs this task for the motive of making money is a hired hand and condemned by God (John 10:13). Payment for ministry is not forbidden in Scripture but the responsibility for support is not in the servant's hands but in the hands of those he serves (Matt. 10:10; 1 Cor. 9:9; 1 Tim. 5:17). For the spiritual shepherd money should be the last consideration.

The third negative is equally important: **Not lording it over those entrusted to you, but being examples to the flock (v. 3)**. Eugene Peterson paraphrases this: 'Not bossily telling others what to do, but tenderly showing them the way.'[5]

Notice that the church is **God's flock**. The members do not belong to the pastor; he does not own them nor is he to control them. The people are responsible to God and it is his Word which teaches both pastor and people alike. Because it is the Word which has ultimate authority the elder will not exercise a dictatorship. Sheep are led, not driven.

But the appointed shepherds are to be leaders, not followers because good leadership is essential to the success of God's work. No one was a better leader than our Lord, nor did anyone have more authority, but he did not 'lord it over' those in his care. He exercised his authority by telling them to listen to him, then watch him and follow his example. As the Good Shepherd he said, 'My sheep listen to my voice ... and they follow me' (John 10:27).

We sometimes refer to 'leading by example' and that is just what Peter means here. A church will be much more likely to follow leadership if they see that the leader 'practises what he preaches'. 'Elders should be those who command respect rather than demand it.'[6] I am sure I have heard someone say that leaders are to be 'models not moguls', and if they didn't say it, I have!

Some years back a friend of mine wrote an article for the Christian press titled 'Stars or Servants?' which raised a few eyebrows. But the church does appear to have too many who are regarded, or who regard themselves, as stars and not enough servants. This is not what our Lord intended. He set us a wonderful example of meekness (which of course does not mean weakness), by taking a towel and washing the feet of his disciples, making it clear that this was to be a pattern for them (John 13). It takes great grace to express true meekness in this way, and it was particularly significant in the context, since the disciples had already had their first argument over who would be the greatest (Luke 9:46-48). At that time Jesus used a child as a visual aid to press home the lesson. 'For he who is least among you all – he is the greatest.' Now in the upper room he loses nothing of his authority in providing this further example for his disciples. 'You call me "Teacher" and "Lord" and rightly so, for that is what I am. Now that I, your Lord and Teacher, have washed your feet, you also should wash one another's feet. I have set you an example that you should do as I have done for you' (John 13:13-15). We need leaders who serve and servants who lead. 'Pastors are to be "overseers" not "over-lords",' says Wiersbe.[7]

The flock has been **entrusted to you**, says Peter. The Greek *hoi kleroi* means an allotment or portion as in the dividing up of the land where each piece was chosen by lot (Num. 26:55). If Peter is addressing officers in the church, it is likely that each one had responsibility over a house church, and perhaps several of these would constitute a city church.

Leadership in the church of Jesus Christ is an awesome responsibility because of that which is entrusted and the One who has bestowed it (Heb. 13:17). I will know whether I am a leader if there are those who are following me, and if they are then I must determine whether I am a *good* leader.

The fact that an elder is to be 'willing' and 'eager to serve' and is not to be 'greedy for money' does not mean that there is no reward for ministry done properly. But the real reward is received when Christ returns: **And when the Chief Shepherd appears, you will receive the crown of glory that will never fade away (v. 4).**

Each shepherd has in trust his own allocation, but all the sheep belong to the Chief Shepherd. Peter had included himself with other elders (v. 1), now he ranks Christ with the pastors. This indicates what an honoured position it is!

The Greek word for the phrase **never fade away** is *amarantinos* from which we derive the name 'amaranth' which was a type of everlasting flower. Peter has already told them that the inheritance which they look forward to will 'never perish, spoil or fade away – (it is) kept in heaven for you' (1:4). Here he underlines that glorious prospect, but with an exclusive crown or garland for shepherds who have fulfilled their responsibilities.

Distinguished citizens in Greek cities were often awarded a garland of ivy or olive leaves but these would wither and the honour would be forgotten. The crown the Chief Shepherd gives will never wither and it consists of **glory** or eternal honour for elders who serve well.

The elders in Revelation 4:10 fall down before the throne and worship the One who lives for ever and ever, laying their

crowns before him. 'The faithful elders who receive their
crowns of blessing from the Lord will cast their crowns before
the throne of him who wore the crown of thorns for them.'[8]

Just a word to **the flock**. Remember that your pastor or
elder is just a man. You are not the only sheep under his care.
Ask yourself, what if everyone else in the flock was just like
you! Be patient and understanding. Don't be too demanding,
and hesitate before sending that letter or making that comment
that may wound him for weeks. Above all pray for him and
encourage him. There is no better way to prosper the Lord's
work in your fellowship.

2. A CHALLENGE TO OUR EGO (verses 5-7)

Most of us have a problem with humility. Peter has followed
this theme throughout the epistle. His readers have been
encouraged to be submissive to government authorities; slaves
have been told that this should be their relationship to their
masters and wives similarly to their husbands. Now he urges
all believers to cultivate a submissive nature the one to the
other.

In the previous verses in this chapter Peter has been calling
for a kind of 'self-submission' from elders, now he says **in
the same way** those who are younger should **be submissive
to those who are older (v. 5)**. The **young men** could be young
in years or young in the faith, but in practice it means less
mature in leadership. Those who are older may not have had
such a good education as those who are younger; they may
not have travelled as widely, but they have what the young
cannot have – experience. For good order to exist in the church
there must be an acknowledgment of authority, and we reveal
a lack of maturity if we are not able to accept this.

The generation gap was not invented in our century, and
the church has not been immune to it in any century. Peter
provides a pointer to solving this difficulty, and now includes
the whole church: **All of you, clothe yourselves with
humility toward one another (v. 5)**.

Some have different ideas on what they imagine humility to be. Proud people obviously think too highly of themselves, but the danger of a false humility is that we think too lowly of ourselves. In view of what he did for us in Christ, God obviously regards us of great value so we are wrong to think that we are valueless. Stuart Briscoe says: 'It is not humility to pretend to be less than God has created, redeemed, commissioned, and equipped us to be.'[9] I believe Warren Wiersbe sets just the right balance when he writes: 'Humility is not demeaning ourselves and thinking poorly of ourselves. It is simply not thinking of ourselves at all!'[10] The emphasis therefore is on thinking of others.

The idea of clothing themselves with humility would have been in Peter's mind again when he thought of Jesus in that upper room, placing a towel around himself and kneeling before him and offering to wash his feet (John 13). The word for **clothe** does not appear elsewhere but it refers to an apron tied on over other clothes. It was a garment commonly worn by slaves, and thus a badge of servitude. Pride doesn't serve anybody but itself, whereas humility is fundamentally a willingness to serve others. All of this is in the present tense which indicates that it is an ongoing process. It is a lifestyle.

A further clue to understanding this important lesson is provided in the verse which Peter quotes from Proverbs 3:34: **God opposes the proud but gives grace to the humble**. Peter now moves the focus to God. Pride is a characteristic of opposition to God. We can never be submissive to each other until we have first of all submitted to God, and *only then* does he confer the grace we need to submit to each other. Humility recognises that we are what we are by the grace of God. What do we have to be proud about? Paul asks 'What do you have that you did not receive? And if you did receive it, why do you boast as though you did not?' (1 Cor. 4:7). He also reminds the believers in Rome that 'boasting is excluded' (Rom. 3:27).

Humility expresses absolute dependence upon God and

so is the antithesis of pride. All of this is powerful evidence of the work of God in our lives. James pursues the same truth when he states that 'the Scripture says: "God opposes the proud but gives grace to the humble" ' (James 4:6). Grace is given to the humble, not to the proud.

This was one of the lessons which Peter had to learn. Pride had been the cause of his downfall. There were times when he had contradicted the Lord (Matt. 16:22; John 13:8), and there were times when he had regarded himself as superior to others (Matt. 26:33). With those characteristics it is surely not surprising that God hates pride! Indeed, says Peter, he **opposes** it. This conveys the image of God lining up his forces against it. Clowney expresses it like this: 'God opposes the proud ... not only because pride despises our fellow creatures, but because pride rebels against him. The proud person sets himself against God, and God, in turn, sets himself against the proud.'[11]

So from his heart Peter says: **Humble yourselves, therefore, under God's mighty hand, that he may lift you up in due time (v. 6)**.

Jesus told the story of a Pharisee and a publican or tax collector who went to the temple to pray. The Pharisee's prayer was a proud presentation of his credentials before God. The tax collector's prayer was a humble confession of his sin. It is hardly surprising that he was the one who returned home forgiven and justified. Jesus said: 'Everyone who exalts himself will be humbled, and he who humbles himself will be exalted' (Luke 18:9-14).

We all know 'nice' people who have a mild nature, though they may not be Christians. The humility Peter speaks about is more than that. It is the humility of the tax collector who casts himself on God for grace and puts no trust in himself. This places us **under God's mighty hand** and there can be no safer place to be. In the Old Testament, references to God's hand often spoke of his deliverance (e.g., Exod. 3:19; 6:1; Dan. 9:15). The individual under the powerful hand of God is not only submissive but is also content and confident to leave events with him.

One commentator suggests that there would never have been a morning when Peter heard the cock crow, that he did not think of the pride which had led to his denial. 'Yet Peter had been chastened, humbled and restored. His pride had cast him down, but his Lord had lifted him up.'[12]

The exaltation **in due time** will be God's good time. It may not be as quickly as we would like, but it will be as one translation renders it 'at the proper time' (NASB), and if that is God's time, it is obviously the right time. Peter introduces this thought to save his readers, and us, from being over anxious in their circumstances. They were not to despair. The hymnwriter is correct when reminding us that 'God is still on the throne and he will remember his own.' Not to trust in God is to trust in ourselves and that is pride!

There is also the danger of trying to make things happen. We get impatient and try to move God along. This too is an open door to frustration and disappointment. Not least because we may activate something which is outside of God's will for us. Wait for him to do the lifting up. It will come **in due time**.

Some commentators believe that it is just possible that the reference to **due time** links to 'the last time' (1:5) – the time when the believer's faith is finally justified (2:12).

So what is the immediate answer to anxiety? Peter's own experience of humbling and restoration underlined Christ's love for him, so he urges: **Cast all your anxiety on him because he cares for you (v. 7).**

I have never been sure about the phrase 'prayer changes things'. I don't believe that prayer was provided as a means to manipulate God to fulfil our wishes, even if they appear to be legitimate. I do believe however that prayer changes people. The very act of casting our anxieties upon him will put them into perspective, and we may even discover that some of them were symptoms of our pride and therefore illegitimate cares. For example we may be disturbed that others are not giving us the credit we deserve, or that we won't get a position we are looking for. This type of 'care' should be cast away, not cast on the Lord.

Having said that, this should not detract from the encouragement of this verse. Peter, without drawing special attention, is quoting David from Psalm 55:22: 'Cast your cares on the LORD and he will sustain you; he will never let the righteous fall.' Cares will come, of that we can be sure, and they can come from a multitude of directions. They weigh us down and make the journey wearisome.

I watched a programme on TV which featured a celebrity learning to be a sherpa and escorting a walking party in Nepal. He had to carry sixty pounds of kitchen equipment and soon realised he was short of the kind of fitness needed for such heavy work. The strain on his back and neck were incredible, added to which, the load meant that he wasn't able to see anything except the ground he walked on. When they arrived at the place where they were to take a lunch break you shared with him in the bliss of allowing that heavy burden simply to drop from his back. But not only was the weight removed, for the first time he was able to look around at the beauty of his surroundings. That is something of the idea conveyed here. Peter says release your burden and lift up your head.

Epiriptein, the word translated **cast** in verse 7, also occurs in Luke 19:35 where the disciples cast their cloaks on the colt allowing it to carry them. Peter is the only other person to use the same word in the New Testament. It indicates a definite and decisive act in handing over our worries to God. A measure of care and concern over various matters is not a bad thing to keep us up to scratch but excessive anxiety, which is what Peter has in mind will wear us down. The word for **anxiety** suggests a pulling apart, which well describes how we feel when we are anxious and weary. To truly cast our care on him will mean that we have a peace of heart which the world cannot give. That in turn may help us to quietly determine what action we need to perform in that situation and then trust enough to leave the rest with God.

Chuck Swindoll suggests the following formula:

SUBMISSION + HUMILITY - WORRY = RELIEF

'Submission to others plus humility before God minus the worries of the world equals genuine relief. It will also provide hope and contentment without the pain of dissatisfaction.'[13]

'Commit your way to the LORD; trust in him.... Be still before the LORD and wait patiently for him; do not fret...' (Psalm 37:5,7).

And why should we place such peaceful trust in the Lord? Because, says Peter, **he cares for you**. This God is quite unlike the gods worshipped by the heathen who were so distant. Stibbs points out that 'Other religions with their many ceremonies are commonly occupied with the business of making God care.... Christians begin with, and are meant to build on, the confidence that God does care (cf. Matt. 6:21-35; Rom. 5:8; 8:32).'[14]

Peter Davids underlines this when he writes: 'Jesus in Matthew 6:25-34 (cf. Matt. 10:19; Luke 10:41) makes precisely the same point that one should not have any anxiety about food and clothing because the God who cares for birds and lilies surely cares far more about disciples. Indeed to carry anxiety is likely to choke the fruitfulness of God's work in one's life (Mark 4:19; Luke 21:34).'[15]

Anxiety suggests that we need to look after ourselves, and betrays a lack of trust in God. In humbling ourselves **under God's mighty hand** we have 'the assurance that God indeed cares and that his caring does not lack the power or the will to do the very best for his own.'[16] However such confidence, while providing for us to be carefree, does not mean that we should be careless.

3. A RECOGNITION OF OUR ENEMY (verses 8-11)

Again we sense an indication of Peter's own experience when he writes, **Be self-controlled and alert (v. 8)**. This is just what he failed to be when he denied his Lord. By virtue of belonging to God's family every believer must recognise that he is in a spiritual battle, and that battle is against a superior power, **the devil**. The term 'devil' is the Greek translation of the Hebrew *satan*, which means adversary or opponent.

There are two qualities which are essential: we are to be **self-controlled and alert** or 'sober and watchful'. Drunkenness clouds the senses and affects our judgment and we just cannot afford to be careless when faced with this particular foe. Christians have sometimes approached this subject with a spirit of bravado which I am sure has delighted the devil. Choruses which make fun of him do not reflect a sober and mature approach to such a deadly foe. It is dangerous to make fun of an adversary. But the devil loves to be underestimated since that is often when he can be at his most lethal. We need to be alert, because he certainly is.

Your enemy the devil prowls around like a roaring lion looking for someone to devour, literally, 'to swallow down'. Don't for one second think that he is not interested in you; he's *your* **enemy** or adversary. He does not even like or treat well those who *willingly* serve him. The devil is not a good master. Imagine then what he feels toward those who must be considered traitors for having transferred their allegiance to another. His aim is our destruction!

Swindoll suggests that we personalise the phrase by inserting our name instead of the word 'someone'. ' "Your adversary, the devil, prowls about like a roaring lion, seeking to devour _____ " He's no sly-looking imp with horns, a red epidermis, and a pitchfork. He is the godless, relentless, brutal, yet brilliant adversary of our souls who lives to bring us down... to watch us fall.'[17] He wants to **devour** us – eat us alive, literally to gulp down. That certainly brings the lesson home! The same term is used of the fish that swallowed Jonah (Jon. 1:17).

Recognise therefore that he doesn't care *for* you but he does care *about* you. He is a fallen enemy because he has already been defeated by Christ, but this also makes him a furious enemy. Having lost us to Christ for ever, he will now do all he can to strike back at God by staining our lives and spoiling our witness. He is looking for any weakness which he can exploit and sometimes he attacks through an area we had seen as a strength. An enemy once took Edinburgh Castle from its steepest side because the occupants assumed that no one would try to do that. All their defences were placed on what they believed to be the weakest approach, the more gradual slope, and they were deceived and defeated. So it is true that the devil can even use against us those characteristics which we believe to be our assets.

The devil is both a deceiver (2 Cor. 11:3) and a devourer. Few things are more frightening than a roaring lion. We are usually drawn to the lion enclosure at feeding time when they are at their noisiest and most active because we can sense the thrill of danger, whilst remaining perfectly safe so long as the bars separate us. Many believers in the early church faced roaring lions because of their faith. Though Peter is not referring here to the amphitheatre, it is as vivid a picture as he can convey to warn of the danger of underestimating our greatest enemy. We should never doubt that God is able to sustain us, but we must be realistic concerning our foes.

Warren Wiersbe suggests that if Peter had obeyed the following three instructions he would not have gone to sleep in Gethsemane, attacked Malchus, or denied the Lord. He should have *respected* the devil because he is dangerous, *recognised* him because he is a great pretender and *resisted* him.[18] He did none of this. He didn't believe the Lord's warning, he was so proud that he didn't feel the need to 'watch and pray' and so he failed miserably (Matt. 26:40,41).

But the gracious warning to Peter included the assurance that he had been prayed for, that he would be restored and that he would be the means of strengthening others (Luke

22:32). Peter remembers all of this when he urges these believers who face the 'fiery trial' to **Resist him, standing firm in the faith (v. 9)**. Never reason with the devil. If we try to reason with him we will be defeated because we are no match for his deceptions. Remember what happened to Eve (Gen. 3). We must resist him, and there is only one way to stand up to him, and that is by using the Word of God and by prayer. Christ himself used these weapons when tempted in the wilderness (Mark 4:1-11). We can do no better.

Both James and Peter offer similar advice. 'Submit yourselves, then, to God. Resist the devil and he will flee from you' (James 4:7). That instruction provides us with the clue on how to resist such a powerful foe – by first submitting to an all powerful God. Peter's experience had been in contrast to that. He resisted the Lord and then had to submit to the devil.

Remember that we have no resources of ourselves. We cannot resist Satan in our own strength. Kenneth Wuest comments: 'The Christian would do well to remember that he cannot fight the devil. The latter was originally the most powerful and wise angel God created. He still retains much of that power and wisdom as a glance down the pages of history and a look about one today will easily show. While the Christian cannot take the offensive against Satan, yet he can stand his ground in the face of his attacks. Cowardice never wins against Satan, only courage.'[19]

This foe can only be defeated in Christ, so Peter urges a **standing firm in the faith**. That means more than holding firmly to certain doctrines. It means remaining firm to our trust in God. It means a recognition of our ultimate dependence on God and an entering into the victory already won by Christ against the devil at Calvary. The good news is that when faced with this the devil will back down. There is nothing to worry about, for he is now faced with a superior power (v. 11). So in the words of Paul, 'Be strong *in the Lord and in his mighty power.* Put on the whole armour of God so that you can take your stand against the devil's schemes' (Eph. 6:10-11).

Peter's readers can also be encouraged by realising that they are not alone in their struggles: **You know that your brothers throughout the world are undergoing the same kind of sufferings**. Archbishop Leighton quaintly observes: 'There is one thing that much troubles the patience and weakens the faith of some Christians. They are ready to think there is none, yea there was never any beloved of God in such a condition as theirs. Therefore the Apostle St. Paul breaks this conceit (1 Cor. 10:13): "no temptation hath taken you but such is common to man"; and here is the same truth: "The same afflictions are accomplished in your brethren." This is the truth and taken altogether is a most comfortable truth: the whole brotherhood go in this way and our Eldest Brother went first.'[20]

Paul wrote to the Philippians: 'For it has been granted to you on behalf of Christ not only to believe on him, but also to suffer for him, since you are going through the same struggle you saw I had, and now hear that I still have' (1:29-30). Both Paul and Peter say: 'You are not alone.'

Others may not be facing identical pressures to ours, but no believer is excused from suffering, because wherever we live, we are in a godless environment. In those circumstances it is a great encouragement to know that in **standing firm in the faith** we belong to a family and that we have **brothers**. It is a morale booster to any man fighting in a war to know that the whole army is engaged in the same battle.

Suffering is a huge problem. There are no easy answers, and Peter doesn't try to suggest any in his letter. Nor does he provide a way of escape from it. He simply tells his readers that they should not be surprised by it and explains to them how they are to face up to it. Part of his analysis is the truth that though God is sovereign and he does test them, the devil is their arch enemy and much of their pain is down to his attacks. It somehow helps to know the reason behind the battle.

It also helps when you are given hope beyond the battle:

And the God of all grace, who called you to his eternal glory in Christ, after you have suffered a little while, will himself restore you and make you strong, firm and steadfast (v. 10). God knows exactly what is happening and why, and Peter looks ahead and gives them hope. These words are a promise, not a wish.

Our first assurance is the fact that he is **the God of all grace**. The word for **all** means 'many and varied types', that is, God supplies every kind of grace. Whatever our need might be, God has suitable grace to meet it. Paul knew about God's sufficient grace (2 Cor. 12:9).

The second assurance is the fact of **his eternal glory**. And since, as Peter says, God **called** them to it there should be no doubt that it will happen! This is not an invitation but a divine summons! Their suffering is real but so is the promise of glory, and whereas the sufferings are only for **a little while** (see also 1:6), glory is **eternal**. Eternity brings the experience of their redemption in all its fulness. Suffering always precedes glory, as it did for Christ – 'Who for the joy set before him, endured the cross' (Heb. 12:2).

Paul wrote along similar lines to the Corinthian believers. 'Our light and momentary troubles are achieving for us an eternal glory that far outweighs them all' (2 Cor. 4:17). When Peter or Paul set suffering against glory on the scales of life there was no contest, and suffering should always be viewed from that perspective. Paul underlines this great truth when he writes: 'I consider that our present sufferings are not worth comparing with the glory that will be revealed in us' (Rom. 8:18). One martyr is supposed to have said to another, 'Half an hour in glory will make us forget all our pain.'

Time and again in this epistle Peter has sought to explain that suffering is not valueless; that it is not merely something to be endured. God uses suffering to draw us nearer to him and to mould us into what he wants us to be. 'The clear object God keeps in view through all that believers face in this world should be a matter for great encouragement when days are dark and threatening. God himself is purposing to "restore you and make you strong, firm and steadfast".'[21]

It is significant that Peter the fisherman uses the word *katartizein* for **restore**, since it has links with the 'mending' of nets (Mark 1:19). His readers must have been tempted to feel extreme weakness in view of the pressures upon them, but God will make them **strong, firm and steadfast**. *Sterizein* means to make strong and the link with today's body building steroids is obvious, and it is also the word that Jesus used when he told Peter that he would be used to 'strengthen your brothers' (Luke 22:32). They will also be **firm and steadfast**, that is filled with strength, and well settled on a firm foundation. These people are secure, they will not be moved no matter what comes against them. Paul encourages the Colossians to 'continue in your faith, established and firm, not moved from the hope held out in the gospel' (1:23).

While writing this book and after some years of lethargy, I have returned to a sustained course of physical exercise or 'working out'. I don't enjoy the process and it can be painful, but it is the only way to regain physical strength and stamina, and afterwards I do feel much better for it. The keep-fit gurus tell us – no pain, no gain!

Spiritual strength is attained in a similar way and the process can be even more painful. Some of the 'all things' of which Paul speaks in Romans 8:28 are not of themselves pleasant, but they 'work for the good of those who love him'. Yes, there is value in suffering.

Peter says that the ultimate goal is that we might share in God's **eternal glory in Christ**. And when he thinks of that wonderful fulfilment of God's purposes, Peter offers a doxology: **To him be the power for ever and ever. Amen (v. 11)**. Again this is not a wish but an assurance. It is an acknowledgment of the awesome power of a gracious God which is the very best consolation in trouble. The **Amen** adds endorsement 'It is so.'

Peter had the great privilege of penning part of the word

of God, but he would certainly have said 'Amen' to these
words written many hundreds of years later:

> How firm a foundation, ye saints of the Lord,
> Is laid for your faith in His excellent Word!
> What more can He say than to you He has said –
> You, who unto Jesus for refuge fled.
>
> When through the deep waters I cause thee to go,
> The rivers of woe shall not thee overflow;
> For I will be with thee, thy troubles to bless,
> And sanctify to thee thy deepest distress.
>
> When through fiery trials thy pathway shall lie,
> My grace all-sufficient shall be thy supply;
> The flame shall not hurt thee: I only design
> Thy dross to consume, and thy gold to refine.
>
> The soul that on Jesus has leaned for repose
> I will not, I will not desert to its foes;
> That soul, though all hell should endeavour to shake,
> I'll never, no never, no never forsake!

I think that Peter's readers too, would now sing this with
great assurance.

4. A PS FOR OUR ENCOURAGEMENT (verses 12-14)

As we have suggested in the Introduction it is probable that
Silas was the secretary or 'amanuensis' who assisted Peter in
the writing of this epistle. It would certainly help to explain
the excellent Greek employed in the letter. He may also have
been the bearer of the letter to the scattered churches Peter
intended it to go to. We certainly believe that he was the
Silas (or Silvanus) who accompanied Paul on his missionary
journeys, and Peter has a high regard for him. Silas shared
many experiences with both apostles and so would have
known both Peter and Paul intimately.

Faithful brothers and sisters are a wonderful
encouragement in the church and not least to the leadership

of the church. Peter may also be implying that Silas will be able to reliably interpret the letter which he will bring to them. Silas knows the apostle's mind on these matters.

Perhaps now, Peter takes up the reed pen himself to add a personal conclusion: **With the help of Silas, whom I regard as a faithful brother, I have written to you briefly (v. 12)**.

Peter says that he has written **briefly**, that is, in a condensed form, no doubt because of the vastness of the subjects he has sought to cover. How could he feel that he had done them justice? There was so much more that could have been said. How often we feel like that when considering the things of God. But his main purpose has been fulfilled, that of **encouraging you and testifying that this is the true grace of God. Stand fast in it (v. 12)**. The major task of the apostles was to bear witness to the truth, and Peter's duty in particular was to do this for the believers in Asia Minor.

So much of what has been written in the letter is Peter's testimony of the grace of God in his own life. He is bearing personal witness. Time and again his mind would have been taken back to his own frailties, and the provision of God's grace in dealing with them. And, says Clowney, 'because Peter's witness is true, his encouragement is real', in contrast to the false teachers he writes about in the second letter (2 Pet. 2:2).[22] As with himself, the position which his readers now occupy is one into which the favour or grace of God has brought them, notwithstanding their immediate circumstances.

So, says Peter, **Stand fast in it**. This is an imperative. Now is not the time to give up. Nothing is to drive or entice them from the ground which has been marked out for them. They are to persevere, to cling on, whatever the outward circumstances might be, not depending on their own abilities or achievements, but on the grace of God alone.

Peter brings the letter to a close by conveying greetings from some of his companions: **She who is in Babylon, chosen together with you, sends you her greetings, and so**

does my son Mark (v. 13). Some believe Peter may be speaking of an anonymous individual, but why should he maintain the anonymity of this 'lady' whilst clearly identifying Mark? One suggestion is that she might be his wife! The **she** may alternatively refer to the church, since this is a feminine noun in the Greek (see also 2 John 1, 3), and this seems the best suggestion. Peter mentions the fact of these believers being **chosen together with you**. This links with his references in the first chapter to them being the elect and chosen of God (1:2; 2:9).

So what is **Babylon**? Though this word was used in the early church as a code name for Rome (Revelation 17 and 18), it surely would not have necessary to be as secretive here. After all Peter has told them that they should submit to their rulers and masters, comments that would gain approval from the authorities! It is however probable that for some reason Peter is referring to Rome since tradition makes it clear that he was executed near there, but he may have been referring to more than a geographical location.

Some Bible commentators suggest that Peter's use of the word here is homiletic, that he is using imagery. Babylon in the Old Testament was notorious as the place of exile. Peter in Rome, as well as his readers in Asia Minor, have something in common: they are exiles in the world but their true home is in heaven. Rome is also the place of persecution (Rev. 17:6) which would make it appropriate to 1 Peter, since we believe the Neronian persecution issued from and centred on Rome. Peter is also concerned with holiness, and Rome would have been synonymous with evil in the world at that time (Rev. 18).

He adds the greetings of Mark. Mark was not his biological **son**, nor do we have any strong evidence that Peter was instrumental in bringing Mark to faith in Christ. This is rather a term of affection in the Lord. It is believed that Peter was very much the source behind the factual information in Mark's gospel, and that they probably worked on this together while in Rome. A reference in his second epistle certainly seems to point to him providing a permanent record of the gospel narrative (2 Pet. 1:15). What we have here is a teacher-disciple relationship. Peter had taken Mark under his wing and expects his readers to know of him.

Greet one another with a kiss of love (v. 14). The kiss of love was normally exchanged between family members and since Christians were 'brothers and sisters' it became a traditional greeting in the first century church (see also Rom. 16:16; 1 Cor. 16:20; 2 Cor. 13:12; 1 Thess. 5:26). The kiss indicated that all wrongdoings were forgiven and forgotten. It was an outward sign which signified an inward peace between believers. The word for kiss *'philema'* in Greek is linked to *'phileo'* meaning love in the family or friendly sense as opposed to erotic love.

Since this act is not as common in our culture, J.B. Phillips endeavours to be helpful by rendering the phrase 'Give each other a handshake all round as a sign of love', but that does seem to lose some warmth in its translation! Even if our culture or temperament 'gets in the way', we probably gather the meaning behind Peter's words which encourages an expression of affection between fellow believers. There may be a good case for this tradition to be reinstated.

Peace to all of you who are in Christ. Peter ends where he began (1:2). It is **peace** from beginning to end and an essential for these believers in their trial. But peace is not simply the absence of trouble and strife. It includes positive blessing and Peter shows that it is entirely dependent on our relationship with Christ; it is to those **who are in Christ**. No one can fully enjoy God's blessings apart from him. Yet all of us can enjoy them if we belong to him.

Since there is no verb used it can be rendered, '*May* peace be to all of you', and would therefore be a prayer. Equally it can be a statement of fact, 'Peace is to all of you'; a final promise echoing the words which Peter had heard from the lips of Christ himself: 'Peace I leave with you; my peace I give you. I do not give to you as the world gives. Do not let your hearts be troubled and do not be afraid' (John 14:27).

Jesus probably said more to his disciples about not being afraid than anything else. And that is the message that his disciples in every generation need to hear, and not least because of the fiery trial. So why should we believe it? Because notwithstanding the fact that 'the whole world is under the control of the evil one ... we know that we are children of God' (1 John 5:19), and as Swindoll says: 'No matter how fiery the trial ... the temperature is ultimately regulated by God's sovereignty.'[23]

Without God – without hope. With God – every hope. 'What, then, shall we say in response to this? If God is for us, who can be against us?... For I am convinced that neither death nor life, neither angels nor demons, neither the present nor the future, nor any powers, neither height nor depth, nor anything else in all creation, will be able to separate us from the love of God that is in Christ Jesus our Lord' (Rom. 8:31, 38-39).

> O blessed hope! With this elate,
> Let not our hearts be desolate
> But, strong in faith, in patience wait
> Until He come.

There must have been many occasions when Peter looked back on his life and thought, 'I wish I hadn't said that.' But what a difference the grace of God makes, and how glad his first century and twentieth century readers are that he wrote this letter. 'Yes,' says Peter, 'I failed him. Time and again I made mistakes. But perhaps this is one of the reasons the Lord prompted me to write this letter, because I have learned things the hard way. I'm writing now from personal experience. Believe me, there is every reason to hope.'

References

1. Chuck Swindoll, *Hope Again*, Word, 1996, p. 223.
2. Charles Ellicott, *New Testament Commentary*, 1897, p. 432.
3. A. M. Stibbs, *I Peter*, Tyndale Commentaries, 1959, p. 167.
4. Warren Wiersbe, *Be Hopeful*, Victor Books, 1982, p. 139.
5. Eugene Peterson, *The Message; The New Testament in Contemporary English*, 1993, Navpress.
6. Michael Bentley, *Living for Christ in a Pagan World*, Evangelical Press, 1990, p. 162.
7. Wiersbe, p. 141.
8. Edmund P. Clowney, *The Message of 1 Peter*, IVP, 1988, p. 208.
9. Stuart Briscoe, *Holy Living in a Hostile World*, Harold Shaw, 1982, p. 197.
10. Wiersbe, p. 146.
11. Clowney, p. 210.
12. Clowney, p. 211.
13. Swindoll, p. 254.
14. Stibbs, p. 171.
15. Peter H Davids, *I Peter*, The New International Commentary on the New Testament, Eerdmans, 1990, p. 188.
16. Davids, p. 188.
17. Swindoll, p. 254.
18. Wiersbe, p. 151.
19. Kenneth Wuest, *First Peter: In the Greek New Testament*, 1956, p. 130.
20. Quoted in Ellicott's *New Testament Commentary*,
21. N. Hillyer, *I Peter*, New International Biblical Commentary, Paternoster, 1992, p. 149.
22. Clowney, p. 223.
23. Swindoll, p. 276.

Study
Guide

Chapter One

1. In what ways does the fact that they are God's elect and chosen reassure Peter's readers in the face of persecution?

2. Why do you think God chooses us in the first place?

3. Outline the assurances which come from the resurrection of Christ.

4. What are the characteristics of Christian hope?

5. Discuss the reasons why God allows, even initiates suffering in the lives of believers.

6. What is the place of Old Testament prophecies in God's revelation?

7. Discuss the differences between 'obedient children' and those who live in ignorance.

8. What are the essentials of holiness?

9. Discuss the concept of 'reverent fear' and its implications.

10. Why would love for the brethren be the Christian's badge of discipleship.

Chapter Two

1. What characteristics does Peter list which will hinder mature growth and what means will help me to grow as a Christian?

2. What are the similarities between the rejection of Christ and the rejection experienced by Peter's readers and how is this contrasted with God's attitude to Christ and to them?

3. What is the church for? Discuss its purpose/s.

4. Discuss the contrast between the Divine initiative and human responsibility in determining the outcome of those who do not believe?

5. What are 'sinful desires' and how should we deal with them?

6. What should be the Christian's response to false accusation?

7. What are the characteristics of a model citizen and what is his motivation?

8. Discuss Christian 'freedom'. What is it and how is it best expressed?

9. How relevant is the slave/master relationship to the employee/employer relationship today?

10. Identify the main characteristics of Christ's suffering and show their relevance for us.

Chapter Three

1. What are the major reasons why a Christian wife should respect the authority of her husband?

2. What characteristics does Peter suggest should be present in a Christian wife especially if she is endeavouring to win her husband to Christ?

3. What balance does Peter try to strike between 'inner' and 'outer' beauty? Do both have a place in the Christian wife and why?

4. What characteristics should be present in a Christian husband in providing for the needs of his wife?

5. Suggest what major principles will determine that a gathering of Christians will be like-minded.

6. What characteristics will be seen from practicing the above principles?

7. Identify the causes and cures in relation to 'taming the tongue' with reference to James 3:1-12.

8. What good advice does Peter provide which might help us to live more peacefully and for longer?

9. Detail the who, what, and why of Christ's death as expressed by Peter in verse 18 of this chapter.

10. What does the physical act of baptism signify? Does it save us?

Chapter Four

1. What does Peter mean when he says that the believer is 'done with sin' and how was that illustrated in the experience of Christ?

2. What is the evidence of 'conversion' or turning around in the life of the believer?

3. Distinguish between separation and isolation. Why is separation the more positive option?

4. What is the difference between the judgment of the unbeliever and the judgment of the believer?

5. What is to be the attitude of the believer when confronted with the uncertainty of life?

6. Why is Christian love a better badge of discipleship than spiritual gifts?

7. Suggest some of the pros and cons in providing hospitality for others. Do the pros outweigh the cons?

8. In what ways can gifts within the church be identified and put to good use?

9. 'Scripture ... points out that the painful trial is God appointed and therefore with divine purpose to test and purify faith.' Find examples in the Bible when that was a case in point.

10. What are the 'right' and 'wrong' reasons to suffer?

Chapter Five

1. List some of the attributes required in those who lead the church.

2. What are some of the essential elements in good leadership?

3. What is humility and what are some of the practical ways in which it can be expressed in the church?

4. What is pride and how does it reveal itself? Where will it lead us?

5. Fear or anxiety are symptoms of the day. How does the Christian deal with them?

6. What tactics does the devil use in his efforts to defeat us?

7. What should be our response?

8. Peter indicates again the value of suffering. What does he tell us this is and what will it result in?